FROZEN,

BUT NOT FORGOTTEN

FROZEN,
BUT NOT FORGOTTEN

An Adoptive Dad's Step-by-Step
Guide to Embryo Adoption

Nate Birt

Carpenter's Son Publishing

Published by Carpenter's Son Publishing, Franklin, Tennessee

Published in association with Larry Carpenter of Christian Book Services, LLC
www.christianbookservices.com

Scripture quotations marked (ESV) are from the ESV® Bible (The Holy Bible, English Standard Version®), copyright © 2001 by Crossway, a publishing ministry of Good News Publishers. Used by permission. All rights reserved.

Edited by Tammy Kling and Tiarra Tompkins

Copy Edited by Christy Callahan

Cover and Interior Design by Suzanne Lawing

Printed in the United States of America

978-1-946889-96-6

Praise for *Frozen, But Not Forgotten*

Nate Birt has written one of the most important pro-life stories of our generation, revealing to parents that each frozen embryo created through in vitro fertilization is, in fact, a precious baby with its own individual DNA. Families that place these babies for adoption are heroes. *Frozen, But Not Forgotten* guides parents through the joys and challenges of embryo adoption—and sheds light on the unintended consequences of our society's embrace of assisted reproductive technology. Like Birt, I seek a world in which each of these children has a home—and in which this book becomes a footnote in history because no frozen embryos remain.

—Nick Loeb, Director, *Roe v. Wade*

I have read the few books that exist about embryo adoption. This book makes a unique contribution: helping people really envision themselves as adoptive parents. Birt helps prospective adoptive parents become psychologically healthy to prepare for adoption, with profound advice on topics such as how to explain your story to other people in front of your children. Anyone considering embryo adoption, or working in the field of artificial reproductive technology, should read this book.

—Daniel Nehrbass, Ph.D., President of
Nightlight® Christian Adoptions

God made life to be good, purposeful, and precious. We cannot deny this fact for any form of life. These precious souls ... need the voice of *Frozen, But Not Forgotten* to plead their case and educate the world.

—Dana Marrs Carrozza, Co-Founder,
Sacred Selections

Nate and Julie showed an immense love and generosity when they adopted the embryo of their little Phoebe. However, it is even more admirable that they have now decided to share their experience. We could write a book filled with love, devotion, and gratitude to life from every child born thanks to the adoption of embryos.

—Dr. Marisa López-Teijón, CEO at
Institut Marquès assisted reproduction center,
Driver of the first European embryo adoption program

Frozen, But Not Forgotten is a comprehensive overview of the embryo donation and adoption process. Written by an adopting dad, it gives the reader a hands-on feel for how the process works, while addressing issues and hurdles that are all part of the journey. A great embryo adoption guideline, and we will offer this to our families as another resource.

—Maria D. Lancaster, President and Co-Founder,
Embryo Adoption Services of Cedar Park

Embryo adoption is simply not discussed in the church today, leading to scant Christian resources and bewilderment. Nate Birt has written a storyline on his family's adoptive process that is captivating. This unique and practical book is a timely resource to equip church leaders and prospective adoptive parents to walk through this confusing subject with sound wisdom.

—Daniel J. Hurst, Ph.D.,
Cahaba Family Medicine Residency

This book is dedicated to the love of my life, Julie, whose purpose and grace have made our family a force for good; to John and Kris Schmidt, whose trust in God and love for little people brought Phoebe and an entirely new branch of our family tree to us; and to my parents, Norman and Anita Birt, who taught me that writing can make the world an immensely better place.

CONTENTS

PART VI: NAVIGATING YOUR NEWBORN'S EARLY DAYS

INTRODUCTION

I fell in love with little Phoebe minutes after her birth. Well, that's not entirely true. I had actually fallen in love with Phoebe years earlier, when Julie and I decided to pursue embryo adoption. But hope had finally become reality. Here in the operating room, underneath a heat lamp, lay a girl whose skin held the blue tinge of a freshly born baby. She yelled and screamed as the nurse tied off her umbilical cord, checked her weight, and measured her height.

She peered around the room with wide eyes. Evidently being on her back provided a good vantage point.

I marveled at it all and kept my distance for a moment, taking it all in. God had answered my prayers for a little girl by bringing me a daughter who has not a hint of my or my wife's genes.

The nurse saw my hesitation. "You can touch her," she said encouragingly.

I reached out and touched her fragile skin, only recently exposed to the surrounding world. She poked her tongue in and out of her mouth in a comical and endearing gesture. The nurse finished collecting Phoebe's vitals, swaddled her, and handed her to me.

I walked the baby a few feet across the room to my wife, who lay under the operating tent as her doctor sewed up her stomach after the Caesarean section. No amount of painkillers could stop Julie's smile from spreading as she laid eyes on Phoebe for the first time and spoke gently to her.

If you are hoping and praying for a baby, I want to assure you this moment is worth every ounce of work and effort you invest along the way. It is worth the worry and the lost sleep. It is worth the questions about what really makes a family and whether you could ever really love someone who isn't related to you by blood.

You might have endured months or even years of infertility. Or perhaps you have biological children and are seeking to expand your family in a nontraditional way. Maybe you have no intention of adopting but know others who are thinking about it. You are wondering how you can get the facts and support them along the way. In all of these scenarios, you probably have concluded that human embryos are children who deserve the best possible chance at life.

Keep reading. My hope is that this book will answer the most common questions about embryo adoption at every stage of the process. Every family's story is unique, so I can't claim to understand or predict everything you will encounter. Instead, I want to share the joys and challenges you are likely to experience along the way from my perspective as an adoptive dad who has been down the road you are traveling.

In the pages of this book, you'll find an empathetic ear and a road map to your adoption journey that is neither judgmental nor overly rosy. If you sign up for adoption, you sign up for a litany of questions—those you will ask of yourself and your spouse, as well as those from friends and family who are unfamiliar with the process. You might find yourself doubting that everything will turn out as you hoped or even be driven to tears. But I want to encourage you that if you use this experience to double down on your commitment to God, to your spouse, and to the family you've always dreamed about, embryo adoption is a magical journey that will forever change your life for the better.

Are you ready to take the first step?

Good. Let's begin. Your baby is waiting for you.

PART I:
THE FROZEN
WAITING ROOM

1

HOW WE GOT HERE—AND WHERE WE ARE GOING

The eternal stars shine out again,
so soon as it is dark enough.

—Thomas Carlyle

In this chapter, you will learn

- How fertility issues affect all US families, even those with biological children

- How in vitro fertilization (IVF) has helped couples conceive while also creating unintended consequences that should be considered

- How your personal journey, like mine, is one that will necessarily expose you to the moral question of what should happen to embryos that are not immediately transferred to a mother's uterus

- How this book will coach you through the process of embryo adoption from start to finish

I don't make a habit of discussing reproductive health with friends and family, much less casual acquaintances. I have a hard enough time discussing such matters with my wife. But I am making an exception for you because you, having opened this book, are interested in building a family. You are interested in having babies. You are probably curious to know what embryo adoption is and whether your own family should seriously consider it.

As someone whose family has taken the embryo adoption journey, I want to help you answer those questions, as well as some you probably haven't thought of. I am holding my daughter in my arms as I write this. (Cradling a baby in the crook of my elbows while typing is one of the few fine arts I have mastered.) As you can imagine, she is well worth every effort. To begin this journey, you must know where other couples have been before you—and where you are going.

Even before we were married, Julie and I had thought about adoption. We didn't know where those thoughts would lead us, and it took us a decade to find out.

Before I share some of the research that will help explain how embryo adoption developed, it would probably help you to understand my family's unique perspective. You deserve to know our circumstances because they are potentially unlike your own. All of us approach the concept of family in different ways.

Julie and I are both proud graduates of the University of Missouri. Our relationship blossomed on campus, at church, and during outings in her tri-tone ramshackle pickup truck. We enjoyed Tiger Stripe ice cream, Mizzou football games (with low expectations of victory, of course), and the sight of the six columns that once upheld Academic Hall in the center of The Quad.

As an aspiringly chaste Christian couple, sex never took a prominent place in conversation around the dinner table, with a few exceptions. Julie holds degrees in animal science and reproductive physiology, so our conversations occasionally veered to include a survey of the unusual mating habits of opossums, raccoons, and other of God's bizarre mammals.

Unusual? Certainly.

Intriguing? Without question.

Relevant to mankind? Not particularly.

As our wedding day approached, the topic of human children took on a more serious tone. We both come from families of four children each and agreed that would be a reasonable amount for our own household. Two would be acceptable. We didn't consider only one child simply because we felt the need for increased socialization and—perhaps more selfishly—another person to bear some of the constant nagging and incessant neediness of little people. I jest (slightly).

We discussed adoption and even foster children, if only briefly. We had some personal experience: my cousin, adopted from South Korea, is a gem. I knew firsthand the joy of family defined beyond the simple boundaries of genetics.

But here is where our lives might diverge from your own. Many couples we have encountered seek information about adoption because they are unable to conceive. If this describes you, rest assured you are not alone. More than six million US couples of child-bearing age—roughly one in ten of such couples—struggle with infertility, according to the American Pregnancy Association.[1]

Julie and I are thankful we never faced infertility. In fact, after three years of marriage, we welcomed our oldest son, Micah; our next son, Titus, the following November; and our third son, Ezra, two years later. We discovered that with each additional child, our acquaintances became emboldened and inquired, cheekily, whether we understand the basics of abstinence. This, of course, stirred my competitive spirit to the point of wanting to continue having children simply to deepen our friends' discomfort. But I digress. It is not a good idea to welcome little people into the world simply to prove you can. It is only a good idea if you have the wherewithal to bring children into the world because it enriches your family and becomes a moral obligation you will gladly bear.

The Bible says Elijah heard God's calling as a still, small voice. We heard no such voice on our journey to adoption. Yet we certainly felt the effects of God's commands to care for one of our world's most vulnerable groups of people—children, including those not yet carried to term—and to do so through adoption. That is the point at which our daughter, Phoebe, entered the picture. She screamed her little lungs out, taking her first breaths in the operating room two days before our tenth wedding anniversary. This was all because of another precious family's experience with infertility and the consequences of a life-creating technology known as in vitro fertilization (IVF).

Infertility has shaped the lives of many US families, including our own.

Although Julie and I have never experienced infertility directly, our respective families had acute encounters with it. Today, despite many advances in medical science and technology that have made childbirth safer, tremendous challenges persist.

Our family's fertility experiences are not unusual, but I feel they are important to the conversation. Let me share two examples. First, my mother suffered a miscarriage before I was born. It is not something we have discussed in detail, but knowing my tenderhearted mother and father, I can imagine the experience must have been devastating. I thank God they continued to build their family, welcoming me and then my two brothers and sister. It is fair to say few experiences have brought my mother greater joy than the art of parenting and nurturing, which she and my father mastered through some incredibly trying times, including job losses, financial hardship, and angst-addled teenagers.

My wife's parents also faced fertility challenges, prompting them to consult their doctor. Through medicine and modern technology, my mother-in-law gave birth not only to one set of twins—my wife and her brother—but a second set of twins six years later.

Both of our families began raising children in the mid-1980s, within a decade of the first successful birth of a baby from IVF in 1978.[2] Five years later, technology had advanced to the point that the first baby from a frozen embryo transfer had been born.[3] Whereas scientists initially focused on fertility treatments for women, later breakthroughs such as intracytoplasmic sperm injection (ICSI) overcame barriers to male infertility and increased pregnancy rates dramatically. IVF has allowed couples to bypass fertility challenges associated with sperm, ovulation, fallopian tubes, uteruses, or other issues to deliver more than seven million babies worldwide.[4]

How Rats in a Laboratory Challenged Us to Define When Life Begins

So while Julie and I didn't directly encounter the impact of IVF on the families around us, we could certainly empathize with families craving the opportunity to raise their own children. To see their sweet smiles. To hear their laughter.

In her laboratory work as a master's student, Julie spent countless hours studying endometriosis, a disease that causes the uterine lining to push outside of the womb, creating inflammation and resulting in infertility. The condition affects roughly one in ten US women.[5] Worst of all, there is no known cause or cure. It is yet another fertility challenge in an era where the zeitgeist suggests anything is possible as long as we put our best scientific minds and technology on the case. For some families, the aspiration of children and the reality of an empty crib are all too real.

Julie never worked with real-life prospective moms. Instead, she and her colleagues focused their research on rats, using the animals to study how the condition passes from generation to generation. She sought to understand the factors that predispose a person to having endometriosis. And she watched generation after generation give birth and die, starting at the early stage of embryo development.

She valued her work and the important knowledge it provided scientists seeking to help families struggling with endometriosis. Yet it also raised a key ethical question: What is the value of an embryo? What some view as a clump of cells is actually a living creature. What is our responsibility to it?

Although rare, IVF creates a beacon of hope for families. Yet its high cost, physical toll, and moral questions cannot be ignored.

As Carlyle's quotation at the chapter's beginning suggests, we sometimes must face the darkness before discovering the light of opportunity. In the case of infertility, IVF is often a last resort for couples seeking a child, and it can appear to offer a bright beacon of hope. The purpose of this book is to show couples, regardless of their infertility experience, that there is every reason to be hopeful because many couples that use IVF to build their families save their remaining embryos for the future. And some of those embryos might join your family one day.

Before you pursue adoption, though, it is important to understand the emotions and the economics that created these children in the first place. For the sake of context, you should know IVF isn't particularly common. In fact, with approximately 1.7 percent of US births attributed to assisted reproductive technology, the Centers for Disease Control and Prevention (CDC) deems it rare, even though demand has doubled in the past decade.[6]

This is not a coincidence. The amount of money couples must spend on IVF is considerable. The chart I've included in the next paragraph features CDC statistics from 2013, the most recent year for which data are available. They show the average cost to patients and insurers. My belief is that these numbers do not reflect another important cost: the loss of embryo babies that are never transferred or placed for adoption.

In 2004, Italy attempted to limit couples to creating only three embryos, all of which had to be transferred. The country also banned human embryo freezing because it can threaten the life of these children. A court ruling later reversed some of the parliament's decisions. But Italy's bold statement highlighted the important point that all human embryos should have the chance to be brought to term. By curbing the creation of embryos never intended to be used, Italy encouraged couples to move away from IVF and toward adoption. I envision a world in which one day, there are no more frozen embryos to adopt because all of those in storage have loving homes, and more couples are pursuing adoption.

Children Delivered	Estimated Cost[7]
1	$26,922
2	$115,238
3+	$434,668

Keep in mind that a good portion of IVF cycles are conducted to help families plan for the future—a future that might eventually overlap with your own. For example, in 2016, approximately 25 percent of cases involved the creation of embryos or eggs destined to be frozen for future cycles.[8]

I will delve into our own placing family's story later in the book. But just imagine for a moment that you are going through IVF—or perhaps you have experienced this directly. Imagine the hours of work and thought you have put into saving for an IVF cycle. You and your spouse are desperate for children. Your doctor and his or her staff will create the best possible embryos using your sperm and eggs. But there is a high financial cost, many cycles result in remaining embryos that do not survive, and there is no guarantee of a baby.

Now imagine you have successfully delivered one or even multiple babies created using IVF. In some cases, it might take six to nine cycles, which can challenge even the most resilient couple physically and emotionally.[9] Then, you still must choose how to handle the remaining embryos, which, from a Christian perspective, are human lives.

Doctors' ability to create and preserve viable human embryos has improved dramatically. In November 2017, a couple welcomed a particularly noteworthy embryo baby, frozen using cryopreservation for 24 years—the longest period on record.[10] On average, families will pay between $200 and $800 annually for embryo cryopreservation.[11] As I will share later in this book, even this is no guarantee these children will survive the thawing process.

You and your placing family will encounter these risks if you enter into an embryo adoption contract. Consider the devastating news families received in early 2018 after learning clinics in Ohio and California had experienced technical malfunctions, resulting in the overheating of storage tanks that destroyed thousands of their embryos and eggs.[12] Couples have welcomed many babies through IVF, but the process can also create a rollercoaster of emotions that last years into the future.

Your Mission for This Book: Consider Reproductive Choices and Their Lasting Consequences

There is not a little full-circle irony in the fact that I am authoring the first chapter of a book about the genesis of life while holding my embryo baby. The late-afternoon sun is slanting through the shades of our basement, glinting off her light-red hair. It curls in the back, a trait partly attributable to the beautiful genetics of her placing family and partly to the fact she has been passed from cradling arm to cradling arm, creating a matted effect not quite ready for the runway.

I am sitting in the cool of the basement on this spring afternoon to avoid the heat of the sun. Julie and the boys are outside with friends, jumping in and out of a plastic pool rimmed in lime green and filled with grass clippings from a recent mow. We live on about eight acres. The cottonwood has been drifting on the breeze, stirring allergies and giving the illusion of a gentle pillow fight from on high. Phoebe is asleep on my chest, her pink owl-emblazoned onesie with daisies lifting every few seconds to catch a sweet, sustaining breath.

Julie and I have four happy, healthy children. We have

reached our optimal family size. At each stage of our family planning journey, we made choices that included following biological, as well as adoptive, processes that brought us here. As Christians, we trust God's providence played a critical role throughout.

In a similar sense, Julie and I threw in our lot in with adoption well before we even dreamed up Phoebe's future. We had a choice to make, and you will too. It will not be the easiest choice. It will not be a choice everyone understands, respects, or admires. You might even question your judgment at times. If you stay true to your moral compass, I can assure you the outcome will be favorable, regardless of what the months and years ahead might hold. We made a conscious choice to forego what for us was the easy choice of having another biological child in favor of a little girl who had been, for all practical purposes, frozen in time since just after we were married.

Buckle up and prepare yourself for the adoption journey ahead.

In reading this chapter, you now know more than I ever did about the history of IVF and assisted reproductive technology. You know that hundreds of thousands of US families take tremendous risks—of finance, of health, and of emotional well-being—to bring their own biological children into the world. And you've also discovered that tens of thousands of those embryos are made specifically to be frozen for a future date. For many, I hope, that future date intersects with your family's personal destiny. To get to that point, you need to learn the process, identify shortcuts, and plan for the long road ahead. It might sound daunting, but rest assured, it is totally worth the journey.

Let me explain where we are headed.

For the remainder of Part I, we will learn about the true unintended consequences of IVF—namely, the vast array of frozen embryos waiting to be given a chance at life. We will also meet two of the smartest people in the United States whose hard work has created and supported a process for embryos to be adopted in a way comparable to any domestic or international adoption. We will learn the basics of this form of adoption, which to most people is a mystery. By the time we finish, you will be an expert, able to converse with anyone about the process and its place in our society, where the value of a human life is increasingly challenged.

I'll also admit something that embarrasses me to this day: I didn't like the idea of adoption at all. The notion of caring for another person's child gave me great pause. I am thankful that my mindset changed. I share how I changed my mind, and how you can, too, embracing adoption as a necessary, rewarding, and Christlike act of service to your family and, more importantly, the world in which we are commanded to be good stewards.

In Part II, we will make a leap of faith by assuming you are genuinely interested in adopting embryos. Together, we will learn what you and your spouse need to know to navigate the adoption process. We will explore how to negotiate relationships, time, and paperwork. Patience will become your dearest friend, and the adoption experts with whom you surround yourself will become your greatest advocates, as you seek to expand your family in an unconventional and misunderstood way. Don't become discouraged. Preparation will give you indefatigable hope.

In Part III, we explore the necessary but daunting task of stockpiling the appropriate funds for your adoption. Many couples that have been through IVF and other fertility procedures use loans, placing their families at enormous financial risk, which I don't recommend. You and your family deserve the ultimate security, and there is good news about the financial aspects of embryo adoption. I also provide practical advice on building bridges with family and friends, even those who are skeptics, around adoption. You also learn how to pray for, and think through, the placing family whose embryos you wish to adopt. Modern adoptions generally are built on a framework of openness, though closed or even anonymous adoptions are important options to consider. Do your research and create a strong match with your placing parents if it is best for your child's well-being.

For those of you with biological children, Part IV is familiar in many respects. In this section, I share how we discovered and processed the loss of some of our adopted embryos. I also explain the process of frozen embryo transfer, as we experienced it, and discuss the stages of Julie's pregnancy that were similar to or different from her previous pregnancies. (Disclaimer: there were more needles and medications than I expected.) Again, if you and your spouse have been through IVF, this is nothing unusual.

Part V is my personal favorite because it embodies the outpouring of love and support we received from so many people upon Phoebe's arrival. From the moment she was born, she prompted questions from loved ones and strangers alike, and her birth has created innumerable opportunities to explain the value of life and the Creator's gift to humanity, starting from a tiny person with powerful lungs and a little flicking tongue. (We asked—her genetic brother did the same when he was little.) I will share some of the funniest misconceptions we've heard about our embryo baby and coach you in how to respond to questions and concerns. I will also share the story of how we developed a relationship with our placing family and met over a barbecue unlike any other at their home. (Spoiler alert: it was awesome.)

Finally, in Part VI, I challenge you to consider adopting an embryo. If you successfully adopt an embryo and give birth to a little boy or girl, you will eventually face questions and thoughts shared by nearly all adoptive parents. I help you navigate those feelings and reshape your definition of family. I provide you with a glimpse of the joys you will share with your embryo baby and his or her ability to melt your heart and win the love of everyone with whom he or she comes into contact. And I help you think strategically about how your decision to adopt shapes your destiny and that of your unique, precious child.

Even though my wife and I have completed our family, we are more committed than ever to providing support to couples seeking to adopt. This book is a necessary step. You see, we have been showered with support from the beginning. Dear friends and family—one of whom graciously agreed to copyedit an early edition of this manuscript, in addition to writing a letter of recommendation to our adoption agency along with two other loved ones—gave us the courage and momentum we needed to persist. Believe me, we encountered plenty of raised eyebrows and doubt. They sometimes came from unexpected places. I like to think that with the passage of time, questions have subsided and Phoebe has grown to the ripe age of two months, where she is able to justify her existence simply by being her adorable self.

The past few years have been nothing short of unexpected. They have unfolded in a way my wife and I could never have predicted. Yet I wouldn't trade the outcome for anything. And I'm grateful to those parents who taught us by their example, rather than the bully pulpit, that adoption might work for us.

It can work for you too. Adoption is nothing short of a blessing in plain view.

Discussion Questions

- Why are you exploring adoption as you build your family? What about embryo adoption interests you in particular?

- Are you comfortable with embryo adoption given that IVF plays an integral role in the process of creating embryos? Why or why not?

- What are you most looking forward to learning about over the course of this book? How will you use the information to guide your decision about whether to adopt embryos?

2

NEW CHALLENGES AND NEW SOLUTIONS

*Peace is the beauty of life. It is sunshine. It is the smile
of a child, the love of a mother, the joy of a father, the
togetherness of a family. It is the advancement of man, the
victory of a just cause, the triumph of truth.*

—MENACHEM BEGIN

In this chapter, you will learn

- How the people who formed the framework for embryo adoption started down the path of helping families adopt embryos

- How the process of embryo adoption has changed over the years and the key lessons embryo adoption experts want prospective adoptive families to know

- Why the process of embryo adoption is best viewed as a sensitive interfamily relationship, guided by a written contract, rather than a commercial transaction between buyer and seller

By the time he was in his thirties, adoptive father Ron Stoddart had successfully launched, run, and taken public a medical diagnostics company in cooperation with a business partner. But everything changed for the California attorney when, at the age of thirty-nine, he had a heart attack and bypass surgery.

He took a year off, opened a legal firm in 1984 to practice adoption law, and has been assisting families with adoptions of all kinds ever since.

Ron is one of several people you'll meet in this chapter, and I want you to get to know each of them for a very special reason. Without them, embryo adoption in the United States might never have been an option for your family or mine. Together, their stories will help you appreciate the historical context of embryo adoption and why families like yours may be attracted to this adoption alternative. More importantly, it will help you cherish the men and women who have made adoption their life's work and who have worked collaboratively with moms and dads, legal experts, Christian leaders, and others to create a path to life for frozen embryos.

Julie and I adopted our embryos through Nightlight® Christian Adoptions. As executive director of Nightlight®, Ron continued to provide domestic adoption services and developed many innovative adoption ideas, including international orphan hosting and the Snowflakes® Embryo Adoption program.

Ron helped two of his friends, Marlene and John Strege, become the first couple to adopt embryos through the Nightlight® Snowflakes® Embryo Adoption program. "There really was no law in the area of embryo adoption," Ron explains. "Although it could be done—we could do it with a contract—embryos were treated more as property than as a person."

Along her journey, Marlene wrote Dr. James Dobson, founder of the Christian ministry Focus on the Family, to inquire about his feelings on the issue of embryo adoption. He later became a major advocate.

Marlene and John connected with a placing family that had been seeking a home for their remaining embryos. Ron worked with the families to develop the world's first embryo adoption contract.

The inspiration for the title of the first embryo adoption program came at Christmastime in 1997, over a musical dinner performance with the Streges at the Lamb's Players Theatre on San Diego's Coronado Island. "One of the soliloquies they did was about snow and snowflakes," Ron recalls. "It was part of that. The guy said a snowflake is unique and a gift from God, or from heaven. Marlene and I were sitting next to each other and locked eyes, and I think both of us felt at once that was the perfect name."

The following December 31, 1998, the Streges welcomed their daughter Hannah, the first baby adopted through the Nightlight® Snowflakes® Embryo Adoption program. Over the ensuing two decades, hundreds of families have adopted and brought to term embryos through Nightlight® and other agencies that have created their own models for embryo adoption.

To Ron, every embryo adoption story is remarkable, even though embryos themselves are physically unremarkable—at the time Snowflakes began, the 400,000 frozen embryos in storage would have taken up the space of a standard board-game die. Yet each embryo adoption has proven to Ron that these remaining embryos are human lives. In 2018, it is estimated that over one million embryos are in frozen storage in the United States.

Still, there have been challenges. Not all people with a

Christian worldview support embryo adoption. A prominent Christian leader who was concerned about encouraging IVF once told Ron the best thing for embryos would be to "thaw them, baptize them, and let them go."

Ron says, "I'm sure, theologically, he had thought through it, and he felt they all would be in heaven and did not have to go through the travails of earth. And there are certainly days when all of us would like to avoid the travails of earth." In the years since, Ron has observed a warming toward embryo adoption even among those who once questioned the practice.

Political tides continue to challenge the practice, though Ron doesn't see any major legal battles on the horizon. The Supreme Court's *Roe v. Wade* decision upholding the legal right to abortion means there is always the outside risk a family could terminate an embryo-adopted baby, despite a contract outlining its commitment to bringing the embryo to term. But Ron hasn't experienced this issue personally, and he prefers embryo adoptions remain where they are today: as an open relationship between placing and adopting families, supported by a contract, rather than as a transactional marketplace where embryos go to the highest bidder. Ron is hopeful that won't be the case with embryos, unlike egg or sperm donation, which have become commercialized.

"The reality is, it is a human being," Ron explains. "The reason we use adoption language is it's better for the child. When he or she gets older, is it better telling them they were adopted, or donated?"

Legislation isn't needed to incentivize future adoptions or protect families, in Ron's view. Instead, the existing framework Ron helped form more than two decades ago continues to serve families well. Those cases can serve as a model for your own adoption story.

"As a parent, your kids don't love you because they know they're genetically yours. They love you because you're their parents. You raised them. All that bonding took place as they were growing up."

In her ten years leading the Nightlight® Snowflakes® program, Kimberly Tyson has seen firsthand a growing awareness of embryo adoption, made possible in part by a federal grant program initiated in 2002.

Despite these successes, Kimberly wishes more families considering donor eggs or sperm worked with clinics willing to share the alternative family-building approach of embryo adoption.

"If you're going to create more embryos with half your genetics, why not consider using embryos that already exist and are simply waiting for a friendly womb?" Kimberly asks. Far too many families she has met over the years have spent tens of thousands of dollars on IVF, failed to have a baby, and later successfully brought a baby to term through embryo adoption. In her view, an important advantage of embryo adoption over traditional adoption models is the ability to bond with your baby.

"It's like a domestic adoption because it allows you to adopt an infant, but you begin the process starting nine months earlier than normal, and you have control over the whole prenatal environment," Kimberly explains. "You're giving birth to the child, eliminating many difficulties experienced by those adopting an infant through a domestic placement."

There is no guarantee families will have a baby through embryo adoption, Kimberly cautions; however, the successes she has seen couples experience, despite initial profound sadness over the absence of a biological child from their lives, points to the opportunities of embryo adoption. Other families adopt even after having biological children, she adds, "because they like the idea of rescuing embryos, having an infant, the woman likes being pregnant, or they've always considered adoption for bringing kids into their family."

For placing families, it's often surprising to learn there are extra embryos from their IVF cycles. "When they're having the embryos created, their focus is laser sharp on having a baby, even though their clinic tells them there is a potential for remaining embryos," Kimberly explains. "They're signing paperwork about their disposition choice for those remaining embryos." They're thinking *It's a piece of paper I have to sign. Let's get on with the process.*

Although technology has improved and may result in the creation of fewer embryos per cycle, doctors have historically created as many embryos as possible because the process of collecting eggs from a woman is painful. Of those embryos, doctors transfer fewer today than in the past, which can also result in remaining embryos. "Then, they're in frozen storage, out of sight, out of mind [for families] until, once a year, they get a bill for storing the embryos," Kimberly says. "The other thing that often happens is that after they have their children from the same set of embryos, their view and understanding and respect of the embryos shifts. They're not just embryos anymore."

In her work at Nightlight®, Kimberly encourages doctors to give their patients facing infertility "each option and every hope." Kimberly herself experienced infertility. She understands the frustrations couples face and is sad that many will never know about this successful adoption option. Use of IVF among families rises up to 4 percent annually, according to data from the Centers for Disease Control and Prevention, Kimberly points out. She expects that will continue as more couples delay marriage and conceiving children until later in life because after age thirty-five, the quality of a woman's eggs begins to diminish "significantly." Even the healthiest women often are surprised to find that pregnancy is often elusive. For some families facing these challenges, embryo adoption may be a more financially feasible and viable option.

"I'd really love it if people would consider using embryos that are being placed by another family because the embryos are humans," Kimberly says. "We believe they are humans, and everything that it takes to make that unique human is contained within that embryo, and every single human started out as an embryo."

My purpose in sharing the experiences of Ron and Kimberly isn't to force you to believe embryo adoption is the path your family should take. Instead, it's intended to help you understand how embryo adoption became as valid a method of adoption as any other, such as domestic or international. It's meant to explain how embryo adoption originated and why couples from all backgrounds have chosen embryo adoption to place embryos remaining from IVF to build families and affirm life.

If you decide to pursue embryo adoption, you should know you are not embarking on a journey where no light exists. In fact, those who came before you and me created a clear and well-lit path that we can take if we decide embryo adoption is right for us.

In the next chapter, I want to share with you why I initially shied away from even considering embryo adoption. Then, I want to tell you what changed my mind. You might be having similar reservations. I want you to know that you are not alone, and you might be surprised to discover embryo adoption is just what you've been seeking.

Discussion Questions

- What surprised you most about the way embryo adoption began more than two decades ago?

- How have the stories in this chapter helped inform the way you think about embryo adoption? What anecdote might help you start a conversation with your spouse, your doctor, or another trusted person about whether embryo adoption is right for you?

- What questions do you still have about embryo adoption? Write down two or three and begin to research them as you read through this book and explore more information online.

3

UNFAMILIAR TERRITORY

·

Love makes you see a place differently, just as you hold
differently an object that belongs to someone you love.

—ANNE MICHAELS, *FUGITIVE PIECES*

In this chapter, you will learn

- How to shed light on, and accept, any doubts or fears you have about embryo adoption

- Ways to face and conquer lingering questions and concerns you may have

- Strategies for speaking honestly with trusted loved ones about your adoption plans, publicly acknowledging worries, and seeking support from people you trust

I'm generally not the man who carries a sword courageously into battle or wrestles dragons to the ground single-handedly. Instead, I'm a coward who does a good job faking it.

This became abundantly apparent on the day Julie gave me mental whiplash. You see, my wife has always led the charge in proposing tough-but-necessary choices that forever change our family for the better. When we struggled to even pay for groceries, she picked up Dave Ramsey's *Total Money Makeover* and spurred us to get our financial act cleaned up (see chapter 7). When I faced the prospect of another exhausting day of work at a company I feared could self-destruct at any moment, she pulled up a college friend's profile on LinkedIn and suggested I apply for a job where she worked. (Ultimately, I ended up launching a successful career that helped me achieve an unmet desire to bring farmers and eaters together to learn from one another.)

But none of those conversations could have prepared me for that fateful day in the basement when my wife's words stopped me cold me my tracks. We were probably folding laundry or doing something equally boring, and I wanted to spice things up.

"We should have another baby," I said.

Now, if you are a husband, let me tell you: If you ever want to make your wife feel really good about having carried three children around in her body for nine months each, suggest that she should try it again, just once more. Make it sound as simple and painless as carrying a laundry basket up the stairs or putting away the dishes in your kitchen cabinets.

If you are a wife, I don't blame you for calling us jerks or worse. Guys understand pregnancy and birth at a philosophical level, and we can be extremely empathetic. When it comes to knowing when to call it quits, though? Well, good luck. Can it really hurt to add just one more baby to your family?

After all, the idea of having four children didn't scare either of us. Both Julie and I come from families of four kids. Being the oldest in our families (myself by 18 months, Julie as a twin by a couple of minutes), we had the perspective to know that big means fun. Big means lasting friendships with your brothers and sisters. Big means only a little more lost sleep than before. Why would we let that minor consideration stand in the way?

I thought I had Julie's number, but in reality, she had mine. Because Julie had been percolating on an idea we had discussed for the better part of a decade. She saw the opportunity to strike, pushing us into unfamiliar territory and laying bare all of my selfishness.

"Can you feel the anticipation building?" she said. "We can have another baby, but only if we do it through embryo adoption."

I know. That's probably not as earth shattering as you expected. It's not like she said, "Sure, we can have a baby, but only after you leap through seven flaming hoops while being chased by a tiger," or "Sure, but only if you drink molten lava while jumping on a bed of nails."

All she said was that we would adopt, and it left me teetering. It wasn't the first time we had discussed the idea, but it was certainly the first time we'd considered it seriously. I can remember discussing plans for our engagement on the loveseat in Julie's old apartment as love-struck college kids. Back then, none of those family planning discussions had the weight of reality. Now, after eight years of marriage, I knew Julie wouldn't back down from a fight. She was serious. We were adopting.

To process it all, I did the only thing I could think of. I hid in my bedroom.

No, I didn't run screaming from the room, slam the door, and pound my fists on the closet. I simply kept my words brief, my emotions cloaked with a smile, and my heart pounding from delirium.

Embryo adoption?

We knew some of our friends had family members had successfully adopted embryos and carried them to term. But in my mind, it was a fringe and dubious practice, sort of like becoming a licensed magician or joining the Essential Oils of the Month club. I didn't mind a bit if other people wanted to do it, but I'd never imagined winding up in the same group of misfits.

Do those attitudes bring me immense shame and disappointment in myself these days? Absolutely. But back then, it was all that came to my mind. I had never experienced the pain of infertility, nor had I considered IVF. I didn't know the first thing about the tens of thousands of embryos locked in a kind of perpetual time warp, awaiting the moment when a loving family would give them a second thought.

Instead, my head and my heart raced onto a completely selfish track. How could I live with myself raising a child whose bloodline wouldn't be my own? What would it mean to never have another biological child and instead go in a direction I had never anticipated? The sense of loss felt immense, and I hadn't engaged in more than a fleeting conversation with Julie. Yet her firmness on the issue resonated in my chest like a bell inside a steeple. She wasn't backing down, and I had a decision to make. We would either be three sons and done or take a tremendous leap into the unknown in the hope of completing our family with a fourth child with a very different backstory.

If you are wrestling with yourself over whether you could ever be an adoptive parent, rest assured you are not alone.

This momentary crisis seems overwhelming. If you give it a little time and a lot of prayer, if you don't mind speaking openly with your spouse through the issues that are bothering you, you'll have a much better chance of reaching a resolution. In our case, we set our minds on adoption and never looked back.

It might not be that easy for you. I had to do plenty of soul-searching myself. If I had to guess, your concerns probably fall into one or more of the following categories. I've listed them along with some reassurance to act as a reality check on these deep fears. If any of these issues are weighing on your mind, I want to encourage you to say them out loud, preferably in conversation with your spouse. You'll never conquer a fear you're unwilling to look in the face.

Here are some of those fears:

- **I might find I'm unable to love a child who isn't my own.** First of all, ownership is a term that shouldn't be applied to children. The apostle John wrote, "Little children, you are from God" (1 John 4:4). It's true that in an adoptive relationship, your child needs a strong relationship with your family as well as with her placing family, assuming you are in an open adoption. Up to 95 percent of infant adoptions in the United States have some degree of openness, according to a survey of 100 agencies published in 2012 by the Evan B. Donaldson Adoption Institute. There are cases, though, where a closed or anonymous adoption is best for your family and your child. Do your research and pray about the decision. As an adoptive parent, you will always be legally responsible for her. Your adoptive child needs to know you are her mom or dad—and that above all, she is one of God's children and of immeasurable worth.

- **I might never have a biological child of my own.** This applies specifically to couples that face infertility. I'm deeply empathetic for what you are experiencing if this describes you. I have never been in this situation, so I won't spend time convincing you I understand what you are going through. I don't. All I want to share with you is that I can't imagine what this must be like. Yet I commend your desire to be a parent. It's my prayer that through this book, I can encourage you that the journey is worth it and you'll love being a parent when the time is exactly right for your family.

- **I might not have any more biological children.** This applies to people like me, who already have biological children but are reaching the end of their family-building days. You might fear, as I did, that you'll never know what other biological sons or daughters might have looked like. You will mourn the loss of that relationship. I didn't expect to encounter these thoughts, but the notion of passing on the family name is ingrained in our families and our culture. If you were blessed to have a loving family, you speak fondly of grandparents, aunts, and uncles from times past. You might have heard, "You have so-and-so's laugh," or "You sound a lot like so-and-so at that age." Don't let these special memories cloud your potential as an adoptive parent. Families are made all the time by bringing two people together from completely different backgrounds and forming something new—it's called marriage. Family relationships ought to be beautiful in part because they are diverse. Adoption can be a celebration of family and a reawakening of your beliefs about how to show love to another person. Set aside your preconceptions and be open to the idea that your family might be about to change in a way that's better than you ever imagined.

- **There won't actually be a baby at the end of the process.**
  This is a legitimate fear, and we'll address this subject in
  depth in chapter 10. As science has advanced, so has our
  ability to preserve embryos in a way that increases the
  likelihood they will thaw successfully. But oftentimes,
  embryos you adopt might have been frozen years or even
  decades ago. Your odds of getting a baby at the end of
  the process aren't 100 percent by any means (though you
  do have an 80 percent chance if you have three frozen
  embryo transfers). Here's where faith comes into play. Do
  you believe each embryo is a life? Are you spiritually, mentally, emotionally, physically, and financially prepared for
  a new little one? If so, you could keep pushing the issue off
  your mental desk for another time. Or you could resolve
  that it's time to act. Julie and I chose the latter. We wanted
  assurance we had done everything in our power to give
  our embryos—however many we might adopt—the best
  chance at life, even if it meant none survived.

- **Adoptions are complicated, involve tons of paperwork,
  and cost way too much.** You've been peeking ahead, hav-
  en't you? Don't worry, we'll talk about shortcuts for all
  of these three issues. Yes, adoptions are complicated. But
  there are plenty of smart people out there who love babies
  as much as you do, and they want them placed with the
  right families. Be patient. Let's not get dramatic. You don't
  need to return to school for a degree in adoption admin-
  istration, nor do you need a briefcase full of Benjamin
  Franklins from Goldman Sachs to fund the endeavor.
  Grit your teeth, smile for everything it's worth, and cast a
  vision for the future. Your baby needs you to bring your
  A game.

When I shifted my mind from a self-centered perspective to a marathon perspective, I knew I'd survive the adoption process. And so will you. I'm no wise man. I simply stole this life lesson from my brother Adam, who along with his wife, Jena, runs and exercises constantly. They have matching workout equipment in their basement, where they charge ahead approximately 375 miles each day. I don't know where they find time to work or sleep or eat Twinkies on the couch at midnight. They somehow get their kicks by being on the move.

I had to drag myself by the ear to reach that point—and it's merely a state of mind. I still don't exercise much. In elementary school, I was the kid who loathed recess. As a way of protest, I'd lug my latest *Goosebumps* book out to the playground and sit under the shaded dome of the twirly slide. Or I'd lean against the side of the brick-encased lunchroom, turning page after page. If anyone ever asked what in the world I was doing, I'd simply take the cue and complain loudly about the abomination of wasting precious class time on sunshine and swing sets. They'd slink away to go have fun, and I'd cross my arms and snort and keep reading.

Somewhere along the way, though, I realized you don't get ahead in life merely by embracing nerd culture because it makes you stand out like a pair of knee-high socks. (Which I also wore proudly, legs crossed, at the base of the twirly slide for a photo op my mom captured in elementary school. Memo to my dad: *Burn the photo.*) To get ahead, you actually have to interact with other people and show that you like them. Along the way, you're probably going to stumble and fall and require them to pick you up again. Then one day, you can return the favor.

That's what adoption is like. It's about starting, stopping, starting again, and ending up better for it in the long run. But if you don't get madly pumped up like my brother and sister-in-law, you won't be in the right frame of mind. You have to want this. Badly.

If you've faced tremendous emotional hardship over the past years and months, you must grieve. If you are resisting your spouse's urging to consider adoption, have deep conversations between yourself and God. But don't for a moment think your burden is too great to unleash. Share what you're experiencing with people you trust. If you're serious about pursuing adoption, you have to heal.

We're all broken. It's a state of being. And as you'll discover next, pinpointing all those broken spots and healing them over will be critical to putting a stake in the ground at the start of the winding path of adoption. It all starts by having your figurative feathers ruffled a little bit.

Discussion Questions

- What are your biggest concerns about the process of pursuing embryo adoption?

- What steps are you taking to confront those concerns, such as having a conversation with your spouse or asking other families who have previously adopted?

- Which of your fears is most unrealistic, and what facts or other evidence can you identify that show you what the truth really is?

PART II:
YOUR EMBRYO ADOPTION ROAD MAP

4

ARE YOU SURE YOU'RE SURE?

Our doubts are traitors and make us lose the good we oft might win by fearing to attempt.

—WILLIAM SHAKESPEARE

In this chapter, you will learn

- Why your adoption agency or fertility clinic has every right to question your commitment to adoption
- Five barriers you and your spouse must address to move forward with embryo adoption
- How to turn frustration into fuel when others question your motivations

Few things in life are better than good cheese. I challenge you to find an experience more transcendent than a butter-laden pair of bread slices glued together by melty, gooey goodness. I grew up on Muenster, but whether you appreciate cheddar or—and I shudder to say this—American cheese, the fact remains you appreciate food that at least has the appearance of a dairy product.

Such thoughts danced through my mind a few years ago as my plane touched down after a visit to the state of Wisconsin, where cows literally work in the state house. (I exaggerate, but you're welcome for the mental picture.) On this particular day, though, beautiful Holsteins and delicious cheese curds seemed a mile away. I busted out of the gate, noisily spirited my luggage across the pavement and made a beeline for my little gray Mazda pickup. I had a phone call to make.

Once I had connected with our adoption agency caseworker, I patched in Julie and we began the conversation. I can't exactly remember all the details, and they really aren't important. The purpose was crystal clear: this would be our final opportunity to bail on the process before the adoption really ramped up. Over multiple phone calls, our agency had walked us through its documentation, explained the time lines, underscored the risks, and invited us to ask plenty of questions.

The seriousness of the matter wasn't lost on Julie and me. We had prayed about it, carefully scoured online charts and PDFs, and ordered books on adoption. We had honest conversations about the risks our family faced by already having three biological children. Many placing families seek to ensure their embryos go to families that, like them, have experienced infertility. Our caseworker explained that families such as ours do successfully adopt, but it often takes more time. Additionally, the odds are often better for couples seeking to adopt embryos from couples whose genetic history includes developmental disabilities or other major medical needs.

You will need to decide as a couple what your boundaries on the adoption process will be.

For our family, we didn't want to make any distinctions or restrictions on the race of our placing family. Nor did we care if the embryos we adopted had been created using donor sperm or donor eggs. Yet we didn't believe we had the spiritual or emotional strength to adopt embryos with an increased likelihood of disabilities. Every baby deserves the best possible life, and we wanted to be realistic about our capacity to provide it. Your family might list no restrictions on the embryos you adopt, and that's extraordinarily admirable. My advice to you is simply to talk openly and honestly with your spouse. God gives each of us unique strengths, and it's in your best interest and that of your baby to know where your strengths end and your weaknesses begin. This isn't a time for guilt. It's simply a time for making some tough and life-changing decisions that will bless your baby, your placing family, and your own family.

We had discussed our preferences with our caseworker, and we reviewed those expectations on multiple occasions. By the time I sped north from the airport that afternoon in central Missouri, we were ready to move ahead. We weren't going to let anything stand in our way.

You will reach that point as well. But before you get there, spend time going through the following questions to identify any barriers that might lie in your path. If one or more of them prove insurmountable, embryo adoption might not be for you.

1. **Are you spiritually ready?** I'm not asking you to don a robe and wander onto a mountainside in solitude to answer this question. Adoption isn't an ordinary thing to do, and it changes your life literally forever. If you and your spouse aren't convicted in your souls

that it's something you need to be doing personally, there are many other ways you can support families without moving forward yourself. Pray for others who are considering adoption or actively going through the process. Donate to a home that cares for children without parents or to an organization that raises money to support adoptive couples. Donate your professional expertise to adoption-related causes. Goodness knows they generally aren't swimming in cash.

2. **Are you mentally ready?** The Bible instructs: "Set your minds on things that are above, not on things that are on the earth" (Colossians 3:2). When it comes to adoption, the law of the land is to do both. Adoption is deeply spiritual, but practically speaking, it requires plenty of mental energy. To meet your deadlines and continue stepping closer to Baby Day, you'll have plenty of work to do. If thinking about piles of paperwork, phone calls, and side steps wears you out, adoption might not be the path to travel. That doesn't mean the door is closed forever. You can always reopen it when your life is in the right place. The same principle applies to families that already have children. If you are looking to build your family but are worn out with the children you have, a newborn won't help matters. On the other hand, if you're willing to accept the chaos of parenting young children and you can check the box on the other criteria I've outlined here, more power to you. A baby might be just the thing for you.

3. **Are you emotionally ready?** Particularly for couples facing infertility, and really for all couples who care about family and having babies, adoption will tug at your

heartstrings at every stage. There's no way around it. You will probably uncover compassion you've never known. You might also discover selfish aspects of your personality you'd just as soon ignore. If the idea of turning over all of the rocks of your mind to discover the rough and unvarnished edges scares you to death, you should probably spare yourself the pain ahead. On the other hand, you should realize a lot of the adoption rollercoaster is self-inflicted. The matching process, which we'll cover in chapter 9, involves a lot of hurrying up followed by waiting. There will be a mad rush to meet an urgent deadline for paperwork or a medical test. Then you'll need to be patient until the next milestone. If you can use the experience as a way to flex your patience muscle, you'll be fully prepared to endure the adoption race and claim the prize at the end. Babies are among life's greatest and most awe-inspiring gifts. There's no need to rush ahead to claim the gold medal. Your little bundle is on reserve for you, for the right time.

4. **Are you physically ready?** This roadblock is probably the most sobering. If you've ever heard stories of people who have prayed for a baby yet been unable to bring one into the world, I can assure you they are true. More US couples are waiting until their thirties and forties to have children, and while the Centers for Disease Control and Prevention (CDC) reports one in five women today have their first baby after age thirty-five, age also presents challenges. For example, as a woman ages, she has fewer eggs, and those that remain are of poorer quality than in the past, CDC notes. Additionally, miscarriages and other health complications are more common. If you are older than thirty-five, don't worry—you might

well be able to carry an embryo baby to term with no complications. Before you make a decision, it's critical to consult with your physician. Come to the doctor's office with questions, particularly if you are the would-be mother: "What risk factors do I face? Would you recommend me as a candidate for embryo adoption? If I faced complications with any previous pregnancies, how can I manage around them?" I would be lying to you if I said everyone earns a clean bill of health. Doctors sometimes advise mothers that embryo adoption isn't safe or likely to succeed. If you receive such a prognosis, know that it is normal to feel an intense sense of lingering loss. If you learn you are unable to carry a baby, we live at an amazing time when families are built through domestic and international adoption, fostering, and more. There is abundant hope, but it might not come in the form of embryo adoption. The loss and the longing are real, but other avenues of hope remain.

5. **Are you financially ready?** Adoption doesn't have to swallow your savings whole, but it will absolutely require thousands of dollars, potentially even tens of thousands. Embryo adoption is among the lowest-cost forms of adoption—assuming, that is, that your prepregnancy treatments go smoothly and that one or more of your embryos survives the thaw, successfully implants, and develops without complications. There are many, many risks as with any medical process. Apart from risks, there are also opportunities. For example, it's common for families to store multiple embryos across several straws. This means you might successfully transfer between one and three embryos, bring those babies to term, and have several embryos left over. Your agency likely will require

you to continue paying the storage fee for any remaining embryos until you decide whether you will transfer the remaining embryos at a later date, which could double your adoption costs, or return them to your placing family, depending on your contract. The process of having a baby in the conventional way is costly enough, and embryo adoption is even more expensive because of all of the steps that must be taken before your big trip to the hospital. So if the thought of costs quickly stacking up is worrisome, that's understandable. But it might be best to consider other options for your family unless you are confident that your savings, insurance, or both will cover your expenses.

None of these five questions is intended to throw your adoption into a tailspin or challenge your decision to build your family. On the contrary, my purpose is to draw back the curtain on the embryo adoption process so you can understand a little of the thought process of your fertility clinic or agency.

In reality, these are not just adoption questions. They are parenting questions.

Nothing will build your character faster than being three days short on sleep, hitting the bed in drowsy bliss, and immediately bouncing out of it to comfort your crying baby. Many newborns awaken every two hours to be fed, and as a tired parent, your body will crave sleep. The experience can feel a bit like stepping on and off of a moving carousel.

But it's totally worth it. Simply put, the act of parenting is sacrificing your own interests. You do this because you want the little person you've welcomed into the world to have the best possible chance of success. It isn't to say you'll never do anything fun again. (Although, let's be real, your definition of fun will shift from a night out with friends to a night with an 8 p.m. bedtime and no interruptions.) You simply need to adjust your time horizon and recognize these moments with your infant are fleeting. If you are blessed to bring an embryo baby into the world, you will routinely be reminded of the wonder of his or her birth story, and of the family that placed your baby with you. The relationships you will enjoy are unparalleled, and you will take them with you for the rest of your life.

Time is fleeting, dear parents. Grab your smartphones and your alarm clock apps and follow me to the next chapter. We're going to work on techniques for waiting on the good things I told you about. Patience might be a virtue, but there's nothing easy about it.

Discussion Questions

- Have you encountered any opposition to your plans to adopt a baby? Is it possible these people are trying to help you think through the barriers to adoption and ways to work around them?

- Which of the five barriers best represents the challenges you will face on your adoption journey? What steps can you take to begin to break through that barrier?

- What actions are you prepared to take to remove selfishness from your life and begin putting your child's interests first? How have you already succeeded in this area?

5

BABIES DON'T
GROW ON TREES

Hope is patience with the lamp lit.

—Tertullian

In this chapter, you will learn

- Why it's best to be generous with your estimated adoption time line
- How to create a mental calendar that will give you a sense of forward progress
- How to unlock your secret patience reserves using missions, distractions, and affirmations

When you are a professional storyteller for a newspaper or a website, time is the enemy. Each day is spent squeezing precious seconds from the clock. Breaking news updates aren't breaking if they're an hour late. Exclusives aren't nearly so unique if two TV stations and the local radio affiliate are already broadcasting live from the scene of the crime.

I picked up on this lesson pretty early in my journalism career, sometimes to my detriment. During an internship with the Detroit Free Press in the summer of 2017, I happened to be posting stories to the paper's website when my editor Nancy (Nan for short) alerted me to a scoop.

Every sign pointed to this being my big break. I'd already earned bravery points with friends and family who thought taking a job in Detroit sounded like embedding with the troops in Iraq. A business reporter at the paper had allowed me to rent space in her basement during my stay, and I'd already made great friends, learned a lot, and toured some of the city's best museums and bookstores. Sure, I'd been heckled walking through downtown. Someone had busted out a taillight on Julie's truck, which I had borrowed for this once-in-a-lifetime experience. But I wasn't about to let those minor annoyances get in the way of a stellar learning opportunity. I was going for First Amendment glory.

That background adequately sets the stage for the big news on this particular day. My editor indicated it had come across on the news wires, and it had something to do with a famous opera star named Beverly Sills. I leapt to attention. My fingers began flying across the keyboard as I prepared to go live with the news. With a few edits here and a few revisions there, I had everything I needed in place. I released my beautifully crafted headline to the masses with the click of a button.

It didn't take long for Nan to recoil in horror at the mistake I had made. She quickly stepped in to scrub the headline and commence damage control.

"Nate, Beverly Sills isn't dead, she's gravely ill," Nan said. "You will forever be known as the intern who killed Beverly Sills before her time."

As Mark Twain once wrote: "The report of my death was

an exaggeration."

Now for the record (reporter jokes, you know), Nan is a dear friend whose mentorship has been invaluable. Her comments were exactly right. They still ring in my head today whenever I am working on a big project and preparing to hit the Send button. Double-check. Triple-check.

My folly is a classic example of a truth that's very applicable to your adoption journey: slowing down might get you there sooner than speeding up.

Ramping down your own anxiety about the sometimes-gradual pace of an adoption will save you from a lot of stress and lost sleep.

Of course, I know nothing about either of those things because I seldom do anything without a lot of hand-wringing. Rarely a night goes by when I get a full eight hours of sleep. My ancestors fretted and furrowed their brows over global affairs and backyard brouhahas alike. There are few things I won't worry about.

You can imagine this served me well as our adoption picked up steam. Once I commit to something, I'm in it to win it. One of my editors jokingly calls me Mr. Speedy. It's usually an introductory clause, as in, "Nice work, Mr. Speedy. Now go and find out about these other three things you forgot to include in your proposal."

Have I mentioned I tend to work with people who are unafraid to tell me the truth? It's an important quality in a person, and it's especially true of your spouse as your adoption proceeds. Early on, I somehow convinced myself that if we got the ball rolling, and then forcibly shoved the ball down the hill, we'd short-circuit the time line our agency had given us. If we developed our family profile, visited our doctor, and signed the agency paperwork, I reasoned, we could have our baby in a year's time.

That's called funny math, and it's only humorous when you aren't the victim. The thing about having a baby is that the baby-growing portion of the experience takes nine months. If your baby arrives early, doctors tend to be concerned. Evidently, I hadn't factored in the actual baby portion of the experience, which is funny considering I had been through the process three times with our sons. Our eldest and family leader, Micah, had arrived two weeks late. Our beloved second son and whirling dervish, Titus, had tumbled out two weeks early. The doctor decided to induce Julie with our happy-go-lucky third son, Ezra, just before his due date. All of them generally hewed to Julie's maternal clock. You can't fight biology. Make sure your calendar doesn't either.

In our case, the correct adoption calendar ended up being about two years. This spans the time we started the adoption process to the time our daughter arrived. You might not like the sound of that. Two years seems like a lifetime, especially if you are a young couple who longs for a baby and who has been battling infertility along with the physical and emotional wear and tear.

Yet there is also hope. Think of two years in terms of landmark dates and you'll quickly discover it could be a lot worse. In just two Christmases, you might be holding a new baby in your arms. In two years, you'll only be a couple of years older. If you opt against adoption today, then change your mind later, you will simply delay the process further.

Keep in mind there are ways to speed up the calendar that don't involve only mind games. For example, an increasing number of fertility clinics are offering embryo donation to their patients. In cases such as these, you might not even go through a formal adoption process. You might simply be able to take the proper tests and medications, based on your doctor's directions, and become parents through the use of embryos donated to the clinic. Still, I feel strongly adoption is best for your child.

I doubt you need me to explain that IVF treatments generally cost more for patients and generate more revenue for clinics compared to embryo donation and adoption. But I'm heartened to hear of more clinics actively moving into the adoption space. Even though it is a not-for-profit center, embryo adoption is vitally important because it underscores the fact that every embryo is a baby that deserves a life with a family. The seriousness of the actions you are taking shouldn't be understated. You are your baby's best advocate.

The next thing you should do is to begin making a mental adoption calendar with actual days, months, and years. This will give you clear milestones to work toward and celebrate. The first few steps, such as holding phone calls with your agency or clinic, completing questionnaires, and visiting the doctor can generally be completed in just a few weeks. As your journey continues, the milestones tend to spread out a little bit more. The process is a little bit like planning your Thanksgiving meal. The veggie tray is easy to assemble in the morning, but the turkey needs to bake all night. In the end, all of the actions you are taking add up to a whole adoption experience that is perfect in the biblical sense—that is, the experience will be complete and fulfilling when the time is right.

Keep in mind that as your adoption progresses, the paperwork doesn't let up, but the reality of what you are doing becomes more apparent. For example, Julie and I started our adoption in the springtime and looked forward to starting the process of matching with a placing family by the holidays.

From time to time, the calendar shifted and it didn't look like we would achieve our goal. Yet the first year ended up closely matching what our agency had told us, even though certain phases ended up being shorter and some longer. It's sort of like leaving the dressing in the oven too long. It's temporarily disappointing, but it does nothing to take away from that beautiful Thanksgiving spread surrounded by the people you love most.

The ability to look out into the future and see where you are going is a distinct advantage. Failure to do so explains why so many of us set bold objectives each year and fail to reach them. You might want to exercise more often, eat healthier or spend more time with your family; however, if you don't think big and use your imagination to picture your future self, you're never going to take risks to get there. Retirement expert Chris Hogan calls this process dreaming in high definition, and I think the same principle comes to any ambitious dream you have, including adoption.

Lucky for you, if you choose to work with an agency, you'll likely create a family profile that puts words and pictures to this vision. The profile is a document that your agency will share with your future placing family. It tells them what you are like. You'll include the story of how you and your spouse met, the hobbies your family enjoys, the personalities of any children you already have, and so on. We wanted to capture our zany country life, so we hired a local photographer we trusted. He snapped pictures of us standing next to the beautiful old trees on our front lawn, laughing while lifting our youngest son into the air. Our favorite image—and one that our placing family specifically told us won their affection because it reminded them of themselves—is of Ezra sitting on a blanket with the family, leaning forward as if in an attempt to lick one of our chickens. You don't need to hire someone to airbrush out life's rough patches, as my grandpa would have said. Show who you are in real life. You might even print some additional copies of those photos and hang them on your wall as your adoption continues to remind yourself why you are doing this in the first place. In the end, it's about building and cultivating a loving environment in which your children can grow.

This illustrates why you need missions, distractions, and affirmations each day to keep you positive and upbeat about what you are doing.

By missions, I mean short-term goals. Maybe it's signing your name on a form and returning it to your agency. Maybe it's calling your clinic to schedule that next appointment. Or, just maybe, it's spending time taking photos with your family and intervening in the nick of time to ensure your son doesn't get salmonella from a chicken.

Every mission, big or small, is important. It pushes you ahead. If your life is a Monopoly board, a mission gets you one step closer to passing Go and collecting $200. The stakes are much higher, though, and that's a good thing. Your life has meaning, and so does the life of the baby or babies you intend to adopt. Missions also ensure you will change. To complete a form, you must print it off, find a pen, read the form thoroughly, sign it, explain it to your spouse in case it requires his or her signature, and scan it in to send back. In that example alone, you can point to all of the ways you showed initiative. You gave your agency or clinic a little more information. You helped them access critical information, and you're now one step further down the chain of events that will lead to adoption. No, you're aren't up to your neck in a World War II foxhole or guarding a nuclear silo. But this is high-stakes stuff. Think about it: You are in a fight to save a life, possibly multiple lives. If you believe what the Bible says about God's care for each person, great or small, you are doing His work. Remain serious on the mission, and have fun with it. There's nothing better than doing work with purpose.

Distractions also are important. You can't always be stone-faced as you move from one task to the next. It might be as simple as taking a walk to your garden, calling a friend, or going to a movie with your spouse. If you dedicated all of your mental capacity to your adoption, you're going to burn out and reach a state of depression. Trust me: I'm the master of rabbit holes. If anything enters my life that is the least bit worrisome, I will fret over it, analyze it, and work myself into a stomachache about it. Distractions are important because they remind you that life goes on in the background of your adoption. Just as you remember your first-and-foremost commitment to your spouse after you have children, so you should remember your spouse, children, work, hobbies, extended family, and other important activities while you are adopting. No one likes spending time around a martyr.

During the course of writing this book, I've fretted to Julie about writer's block, anxiety that no one will read what I've put to paper, fears that I'll make a mistake and so on. Her graceful response has been, "You're not the only one who did this adoption thing." She's right. You have a whole host of people supporting you, fighting for you, and looking out for your best interests. But there's a catch. To let them help you, it's necessary to open a door to your life. You don't need to be an overly open book who muses publicly about the many fears and reservations you have. At the same time, you shouldn't shy away from talking with a handful of people you trust deeply who can listen with empathy and share ideas and insights that might encourage you and make you stronger. Seek out distractions and people with whom you can enjoy them.

Those individuals can also help you with the third and final aspect of my formula for keeping you sane as you contemplate the daunting adoption calendar. That is, they can provide you with affirmations. An affirmation is simply a statement of belief and support that helps you recall why you are doing what you are doing. When you surround yourself with loved ones, they will naturally offer affirmations that point you toward true north. They might not fully appreciate what you are experiencing as a soon-to-be adoptive parent, but they know you well enough to honestly say you mean a lot to them. As such, they will do anything in their power to shoulder some of your weight along the way. Naturally, they'll expect you to do the same for them in the days ahead.

Adoption is a journey that will require you to stay focused even as you are tempted to shirk responsibilities, give up, or back down. Do none of those things. Instead, use the calendar as a practical way to peer into the amazing future God has in store for you. More importantly, use the calendar as a mechanism to peer into your child's incredible future. I view my own children as a telescope into the future where I see high school graduation ceremonies, weddings, and grandchildren. God doesn't give any of us a signed contract that those things will eventually happen. Tragedy and age and dozens of other factors are constantly hampering loving families' plans for the future.

But if you never dream, you'll never realize what might be. You'll never have a full appreciation for the joy of every waking moment. My hope for you is to have all of those things. Cast a vision for the future. And be on the lookout for a big old machete. You're going to need it to whack through a whole bunch of paperwork on your family's behalf in the next chapter.

Discussion Questions

- What does your ideal adoption calendar look like, and what does a more realistic version look like? Are you comfortable with the idea your calendar will likely change?

- What are the next three milestones on your adoption journey? Right them down on a piece of paper, include the date on which you plan to achieve that goal, and post the paper in a prominent place such as your refrigerator or your office. You and your spouse can use this sheet of paper as a rallying cry for your adoption whenever things get tough.

- What are some specific ways you can ensure your journey includes plenty of missions, distractions, and affirmations? Who among your circle should you bring on the journey?

6

BECOME YOUR BEST (AND MOST ORGANIZED) ADVOCATE

Just as the oak tree develops from the germ that lies in the acorn, and the bird develops from the germ that lies asleep in the egg, so will your material achievements grow out of the organized plans that you create in your imagination.

—Napoleon Hill

In this chapter, you will learn

- How to persist while looking for the right information in the right places, even when it's uncomfortable

- How to be extremely polite yet firm

- How you can channel the attributes of the best journalists to keep track of appointments, phone calls, and paperwork

- How to strategize and receive the timely information you need

As a cub reporter at the *Columbia Missourian* newspaper, I became a little bit famous. No, I wasn't the most talented investigator or skilled writer. Instead, I created my own version of a Rolodex wedged inside a black plastic binder. My list of contacts eventually outgrew the binder, so I did what any good journalist would do: I simply kept stuffing new name cards into their alphabetized positions.

When a story broke about someone who had been arrested or who was to be tried—you can guess that I covered the cops and courts beat—I could simply whip out my little black book from a backpack or its place next to the phone, dial up a prosecutor, overcome my nervousness, and ask my questions. They weren't always the right questions. As a university sophomore, I still had plenty to learn. But the little black book served as my anchor. It helped me find the right people and ready myself for tough conversations.

If you plan to adopt embryos, you need to prepare to ask—and answer—similarly tough questions. Your family's future depends on it. You will need to summon the courage to be your own best advocate. It's not necessary to drop everything and find the nearest newsroom. You don't need to build a comprehensive list of all the movers and shakers in your community to get to the answers you need either. You simply need to channel the spirit of an intrepid, enthusiastic, and curious reporter because it will allow you to ask the right questions and find the best answers on your adoption journey.

You see, the little black book didn't just contain names, titles and phone numbers. It wasn't purely a record of email addresses and times when my life has intersected with others' lives. I also made sure that occasionally, the book contained a note or two about something in each person's life that would help me relate to him or her instantly. Perhaps I had written a comment on a person's children or hobbies. Or perhaps I wrote a warning that someone had acted rudely and I needed to tread lightly.

There is practical value in knowing how to connect with someone and letting him or her know that you cared enough to remember those details. By seeking to learn about the people who will help your adoption journey, you will provide yourself with valuable information. More importantly, you will build lasting relationships that will be meaningful to your adopted child specifically and your family generally as he or she grows up. You will be able to point to examples of specific people who helped facilitate your baby's arrival into the world. Store those details in your memory or, if your memory is as porous as mine, use your smartphone to record important details.

Let me stress that this seems silly at first. You will not understand why it matters to write the name of your OB/GYN's secretary's beloved Westchester terrier. But I can assure you that the more people you meet throughout your adoption experience and the more papers you complete, the more scattered your memory becomes. It isn't a reflection on you as a person or your inability to keep up with the basic necessities of life. It is simply a reflection that, in a busy world going in a hundred directions, your ability to recall meaningful anecdotes about others will cut through the noise and highlight your genuine interest in their well-being.

Practice persistence as a means of reaching your adoption goals.

Many people think that annoying is a suitable synonym for persistent. You might be one of them. This isn't a judgmental statement. It's simply a reflection of the fear of confrontation that seems to stem from our Puritanical values of hard work and independence. If I have to ask for something, I am weak. If I have to ask twice, I am a pest.

I want you to think about it in the context of seeking information as you move through the process of adoption. Keep in mind what adoption is at its core. It is an effort to expand your family by extending love, grace, and affection to another person, and in turn his or her family, because it is the right thing to do. More than that, adoption can best be viewed as a moral imperative. You have every right to be politely pushy.

In his book *Adopted for Life*, Russell Moore makes a compelling argument that adoption is necessarily countercultural and inherently Christian. It affirms life and the broad tent of relationships that add up to a family in a world where genetic lineage is too often viewed as the only factor that matters. Never forget the virtue of adoption. At the same time, remember that you are not in this for praise, accolades or a higher ranking on the heavenly scoreboard. If I know you at least a little, and I think I do, you are doing this because you love children, and you feel compelled to make a difference in the world—yours and theirs.

"When we adopt—and when we encourage a culture of adoption in our churches and communities—we're picturing something that's true about our God," Moore writes. "We, like Jesus, see what our Father is doing and do likewise (John 5:19). And what our Father is doing, it turns out, is fighting for orphans, making them sons and daughters."

Consequently, you must place your desire to adopt firmly on a foundation of persistence. Jesus tells a story that illustrates the point nicely. In Luke 11:5–10, he presents his disciples with a scenario in which a man approaches his friend at midnight. If you are young and energetic, perhaps this resonates with you because you are awake at all hours of night with no effect on your ability to earn a living the next day. For those of us approaching middle age, this story is exhausting without further detail. Who wants to be disturbed from a deep sleep in the middle of the night, even if a friend is the one on the other side of the deadbolt?

Nonetheless, Jesus says, this friend comes to the door and asks for three loaves of bread. As it turns out, the friend is hosting a guest and has an empty pantry. Now, if this were my friend, I would question why he didn't prepare. My wife and I live on about eight acres, we garden, and we tried over the past couple years to plant trees and bushes that yield some kind of sustenance. Shouldn't this friend have extra food? Wasn't the grocery store open just a few hours ago? Was this really as big of a surprise as your friend claims? (As you can tell, I'm a really nice friend. If it weren't for my wife, who helps our family foster and maintain relationships, I'd become a hermit, disappearing into the woods to grumble to the rabbits about moral decay and the decline of common sense.)

Jesus' story concludes with the happy ending that the homeowner begrudgingly responded to his friend's plea. But the interesting thing for you to note as an adoptive parent is that the sleepy man doesn't hand out food because of an existing relationship. Not at all. Instead, Jesus says, the homeowner handed over the bread and whatever else the friend needed (butter and a little garlic?) because of the friend's impudence. Other versions say it this way: the homeowner helped his friend because of his friend's *persistence*.

Think about that for a moment. Persistence can be your greatest ally, and if you are reading this book, chances are good you already have amount of it. Jesus, of course, speaks of the virtue of persistence while pursuing things that aid spiritual development. An ardent disciple must ask the right questions and keep seeking answers until he or she is satisfied. If you already have children, you know persistence is necessary to remain strong through days when you'd rather just acquiesce. And if you are faced with infertility yet determined to become a parent, you absolutely understand the notion of persistence. Every obstacle and barrier represents yet another opportunity to fight through the pain, physical and emotional, for the reward you are convinced lies on the other side.

Use the adoption process to foster a culture of caring while seeking key information.

I have already acknowledged that I do not equate persistent people with annoying people. I don't mean, though, that persistence requires you to treat others poorly. Let me give you an example: I was at a restaurant recently and one of my companions, a picky eater, began sparring with the waiter over the menu. It wasn't a deliberate assault on the waiter's family heritage, core values, or competencies. But it certainly felt that way. My companion had crossed a line.

Here is why persistence can be misconstrued as meanness. If you are emotionally tangled in an issue such as adoption, the stakes—especially in your mind—are extremely high. Fatalistic thinking emerges rather quickly. For example, you might think to yourself, if this person doesn't respond to my email immediately, I am going to assume he or she hates me, he or she hopes my adoption is unsuccessful, and I will never be a parent.

Back to the restaurant. My companion didn't think directly about the demanding tone she used. Asking questions about the food on a menu is completely OK. The challenge becomes raising such questions and engaging in those conversations while preserving your dignity and that of the person with whom you are speaking.

Now, let's connect these observations with adoption. By this point, you have embraced the notion of embryo adoption, set a realistic time line, and prepared yourself for the many steps necessary to welcome your baby home. If you accept the seed of no other ideas that I give you, please accept this one: choose kindness in all of the relationships you foster as you walk through the stages of adoption. This positive energy will uplift you when you are discouraged, buoy your spouse's hopes, and increase the odds the adoption experts in your life will enjoy working with you. And you never know when you might find yourself needing a favor from someone who might otherwise decline to perform that favor.

You should never be ashamed of persistently and kindly asking the right questions because persistence and kindness are attitudes that come naturally to parents. Whether you are a longtime parent or a first-time parent, this disposition is something you will need to nurture and grow over a period of decades until your child leaves home. It is not simply a skill you will use for a few months and then discard in favor of a harsher, more hostile position.

Consider this scenario. Imagine yourself in a decade. Your beautiful embryo baby is now a ten-year-old in the fifth grade, and he is struggling in class. His teacher realizes this and considers calling you at home early in the school year to alert you. Instead, the teacher avoids the call. It turns out your child can't see the board and needs glasses. But because your child didn't reveal his struggle and no intervention happened, his grades have suffered. By the end of the semester, it's too late to help your child improve. Did conflict avoidance help? Not at all. A little persistence would have spared significant (perhaps even literal) headaches for your child.

In a similar way, you must be your own best advocate to ensure the adoption process goes smoothly. Unless you are working with a well-heeled adoption agency and hundreds of employees—and I am aware of no agency that matches these criteria—your family will not attract exclusive attention. This is no reflection on the quality of compassionate service rendered daily, amid long hours and stressful situations, by adoption agencies everywhere. Instead, it is merely reality to state that agencies have finite resources to provide extensive one-on-one care to prospective parents. As a result, if you can navigate the world of the agency, the odds are better that you will get answers you need without fracturing your relationship with the agency.

To ensure this relationship remains strong, get to know the people with whom you interact at your agency. When you began the adoption process, you probably contacted someone at an agency based on some content from a website, or newsletter, or Facebook post. It probably sparked a brief email conversation or a fifteen-minute phone call. And while you might continue with deeper conversations with that person a few more times, chances are good your adoption request will move to other people. Still, don't forget the first person you contacted about your interest in adoption. He or she is likely a ready reference for everything you will need on your journey and might be able to help you find the right experts and information sources if you hit a roadblock.

At other times, you will need to branch out. For example, some people have greater experience with embryo adoption while others are better versed in international adoption. Learn the specialties of each, and consider how they can inform your own journey. Admittedly, some peoples' personalities naturally align more with your own, while other people might be difficult to work with. Perhaps they do not answer your questions within 24 hours as another agency expert did. Or maybe their responses to your questions are shorter or seemingly terser than those of another person.

You should view these differences unemotionally. Don't make the same mistake I did. Julie knows that when I send a lengthy email, or leave a lengthy voicemail, I generally expect an equally thoughtful response. But life isn't that simple, and—as I have already noted—time is particularly finite at an adoption agency that is taxed in a thousand different ways. If you receive a response that satisfies your questions, no matter the length or the artfulness with which it was composed, or the apparent kindness of the salutation, accept it with gratitude. Keep in mind that this is only one of many interactions with the agency. The agency is there to help. Both of you are now one step closer to bringing a baby into the world because of the care and tact you show with each, interaction, no matter how fleeting.

Always reciprocate kindness, and always choose to demonstrate compassion even if your store of it exhausted. I assure you, the currency of compassion carries you further than any check you write during the adoption process. With today's commonly recommended practice of open adoption, the odds are good you will interact with your agency friends for months and even years. Build a lasting foundation. It means the world to your child.

Act and think like a journalist to develop positive relationships and maintain productive correspondence.

Now, I am going to teach you to use the skills of a reporter to build close relationships during your embryo adoption and maintain an open dialogue with the experts who are supporting your family. I am of the opinion that this will give your family tremendous peace of mind.

To develop strong relationships, you must first look inward. Does your good reputation extend beyond people who know you best to include casual acquaintances such as those in your faith community, those with whom you work, or those who are your neighbors? In the months ahead, you will be meeting with a caseworker who will probe your mind, and that of your wife and children (if you have any) deeply as he or she seeks to understand your motivations for adoption and your household's environment. You want to exude genuine confidence during that process, and part of that involves ensuring your relationships with others are healthy. You will have a difficult time defending your credibility as a prospective parent if your relationships far and near are in tatters. And as Scripture suggests, your sins, even if they are as seemingly petty as a bad attitude or a proclivity for unkind words, will find you out.

The other critical skill you must have as an adoptive parent is the ability to nurture productive conversations to keep open channels of correspondence among you, your adoption agency, and other experts who are helping you. One of the key difficulties in the adoption process is a loss of momentum. You have completed all of the necessary paperwork, answered phone calls from your agency, obtained background checks, etc., and then suddenly everything just stops. Where did everyone go? Did the agency suddenly stop caring about me and my insatiable desire to become the world's No. 1 dad? Absolutely not. Recall our earlier point. Adoption agencies are comprised of people just like you and me. They have more work and responsibilities than they have time. So it is your job to initiate the check-in.

As a reporter, I have frequently encountered a problem

with which you are probably equally familiar: the unanswered email. You can read a thousand reasons into unresponsiveness, but the fastest way to dispel your assumptions and reach the truth is to take the first step. My editors always advised me to pick up the phone and just make the call. It isn't comfortable, and you're likely going to swallow your pride and a little fear. But a phone ringing in a person's office is bound to attract attention, whereas an email quickly becomes buried.

I don't mean that you should call your agency three times a day and leave increasingly hostile voicemails. However, if you haven't received an answer in 48 hours, it doesn't hurt to pick up the phone. Or if the phone makes you uncomfortable, send a brief (and I mean brief—keep it to two or three sentences) email as a reply to your previous email. This shows the person that you are genuinely seeking his or her answer to a question of genuine importance and that you have been polite enough to delay sending a note until a reasonable amount of time has passed. In a very real sense, you are your agency's customer. The agency doesn't owe you a thing, but as an agency, whose mission is to serve children and families, it's team members desire to keep in touch with you just as much as you seek to have a relationship. I can assure you that as soon as the person is able to do so, he or she will respond, either by phone or in writing.

Keep in mind the response won't always be your ultimate answer. You might get a response that says, "Thank you for checking in. Unfortunately, we have had some team members out of the office, and we need a day or two more to process your response. We will let you know just as soon as we have more concrete information." Please see this as a minor victory, not a loss. You have obtained some information—and some is better than none—and you know when to expect a more informative reply. Take solace knowing that other families just like you are experiencing the same lag time. With these skills I am teaching you, you should have greater peace of mind because you know how to navigate the process and what challenges are normal.

When Julie and I were going through this process, I made use of two techniques that might be helpful to you. One is to send your email inquiry at a time when you can reasonably expect to get a reply. I prefer sending important emails in the mornings because they will appear at the top of the recipient's inbox. It is also more likely the person you are querying will have time to respond that same day. By that same logic, early to midweek emails are better than those sent on Fridays. Set your adoption team up for success. The other technique is to search your email for the last correspondence you sent that person. Simply click the "reply" button on that message so the recipient can review all of the emails up to this point. Your adoption agency handles many requests, and you can't expect them to remember your specific request, much as they might like to, without helpful prompts.

While you are developing your relationships and remaining persistent as you communicate with your agency, remember that a good journalist always keeps an eye on the calendar. This is a necessary part of any goal you set. If you want results, you need to have a target date in mind. The adoption isn't always easily navigated, and in chapter 5, we discussed the importance of setting a realistic time frame. But as an adoptive parent, you have a responsibility to keep the calendar in mind for the sake of your family. Adoption affects everyone in your circle, not just you individually. You know your calendar better than anyone, and you share it with your agency and other experts who are helping you. In this way, you can help your family meet its goals.

One specific time when you need to have your schedule planned well is your embryo transfer. Specific medications must be taken at specific times, and you must complete specific contracts to ensure your embryos are shipped to your home clinic in preparation for the transfer. As the weeks leading up to your transfer approach, prioritize responding to calls and emails related to the transfer process. Read every document carefully, understand your legal responsibilities, and provide all necessary signatures and details. Look ahead to the next two or three stages of the embryo adoption process to understand how your actions today will have ripple effects into the future.

The best-case scenario is that everything happens exactly as expected. The worst-case scenario is that a delay—due either to your fault or another stakeholder's—occurs. A delay at the transfer stage drastically slows the process, for example, because your clinic likely only conducts frozen embryo transfers at certain times of each month. Don't become discouraged; simply understand the spectrum of outcomes and work to control the things within your power. If you are a Christian like I am, prayer has tremendous outcomes. I highly encourage it.

Think through your words, spoken and written, to ensure responsiveness.

I want to leave you with a final thought that I hope is empowering: your words matter. Not only is it important that you have a voice, but also it is important that your words move other people to action. I put this approach to use in particular in emails. For example, if some time had elapsed since the agency had updated me, I made a habit of sending a polite note. It might look something like this:

Dear agency team member,

I hope this finds you having a wonderful week. Julie and I are so grateful for all of the help you have provided this month as we prepare for the next stage of our embryo adoption.

I wanted to follow up to see if you had any updates to share ahead of our meeting with our caseworker? I know one of the things our caseworker is likely to ask is the status of our adoption, and I wanted to be able to share any updates with her at that time.

Thank you very much for your time and any information you might be able to share. I hope you have a great afternoon, and we look forward to hearing from you soon.

Sincerely,

Nate

You might think that language is a little formal, and that is perfectly fine. But I have always found that a professionally worded message gets a better and more prompt response than a sloppy one. Of course, adoption agency team members are wonderful people. But keep in mind they encounter many people every day, many of them understandably emotional and faced with life-changing issues, such as infertility, family planning, and health-care changes. (You can imagine that mothers taking medicine to prepare for embryo transfer have a difficulty managing the resulting hormonal changes, and fathers have challenges managing emotions during the process, so it is a big task for your agency. Treat its employees with the respect they deserve.)

By sending an email, you are effectively knocking lightly on their office door, peeking your head in and asking to borrow a minute of their time. Don't be harsh or abusive. That won't get you anywhere, and it will douse the bridge you are hoping to build with gasoline. Simply and clearly state that you are hoping for timely answer, explain why you need the information, and thank them profusely for their time.

You might think your agency or the other experts you encounter during the adoption process view you as yet another faceless figure in a sea of demanding, griping people. Reframe your perspective. By embracing the thought processes of a good reporter, who can build relationships quickly and acquire valuable information, you can bring a breath of fresh air into the lives of those around you. Your adoption process can be a journey in which others you've never known quickly become your greatest allies. Some might even become your friends.

Discussion Questions

- How comfortable are you in relationships where conflict is unavoidable? How will you and your spouse adapt to the need for healthy conflict as your adoption journey continues?

- Think of an experience in your life where persistence paid off. What steps did you take to achieve your goal without becoming a pest?

- How can you bring a compassionate attitude to the new relationships you are building with your adoption agency and other experts to ensure your adoption proceeds successfully?

- What are three clear steps you can take this week to become better organized as your adoption process becomes more complicated?

- Identify a goal in each of the following: 1) developing positive relationships and 2) maintaining productive correspondence

- Based on what you have read in this chapter, what is one technique you will attempt to use to ensure you obtain the answers you need from your agency team or other experts in a timely way?

PART III:
THE MATCH

7

BIG CHECKS AND CHUBBY CHEEKS

The lack of money is the root of all evil.

—MARK TWAIN

In this chapter, you will learn

- Why financial security is an important building block for your baby's future
- How you can take practical steps to get out of debt and cash-flow your adoption
- Why financial freedom is a gift that will repay your family dividends that no other investment can return

The birth of my oldest son, Micah, forever changed how I think about money. Julie and I were living in St. Louis at the time. We were making the best money we had ever seen. Yet we were completely and utterly broke.

Parenting a newborn quickly exposes the flaws in your game plan. When we brought Micah home from the hospital back in June 2010, we couldn't have been happier. My employer provided two weeks of paid paternity leave, ensuring we wouldn't miss out on paying for rent or utilities. More than that, it provided quality bonding time with my wife and son. Despite those opportunities, it quickly became apparent that we were living on a bubble.

Most of our friends lived about 20 minutes away, and the church building where we worshiped stood an equal distance away. Our monthly bill to put gas in the car grew astronomically. To make matters worse, we so poorly managed our finances that we ended up putting groceries on our credit card. The thing about groceries is that you need them every week. You can imagine how our outstanding bill got larger rather than shrinking into oblivion.

The looming weight of a modest credit-card bill would have been sufficient to strain our marriage. But its effects seemed outsized because of a related financial dilemma: student loans approaching $100,000. Few things in life are scarier than watching as bills from the federal government and private lenders pour into your mailbox and email inbox month after month. It leaves you with the impression you are simply treading water until something bad happens, and then you will really be in a jam.

We knew we needed to change, but Julie understood we needed a plan to have any chance of success. She picked up a copy of Dave Ramsey's *The Total Money Makeover* at the library, read it within days, and encouraged me to do the same. In our hands, we held the secret sauce to changing our trajectory and building a life of freedom for Micah and any other children we would have. Now came the difficult work of putting our knowledge to work and making the painful sacrifices that would be required to win with money.

Whether you adhere to Dave's financial guidelines or another expert resource, the basis of your financial plan should be this: create an emergency fund, get out of debt, and pay cash for your adoption.

It sounds like a simple no-brainer, but my experience proved to me it takes tremendous discipline. If you've ever read *Total Money Makeover* or listened to Dave on the radio, you know the first of his seven Baby Steps is to set aside an emergency fund of $1,000.

Guess what? We scrimped, saved, clawed, and cut back on spending at every turn. It still took us a year to get that fund established. If you haven't already begun to set aside cash for a rainy day, there's no question in my mind today is the day to get started.

An emergency fund is practical because it ensures that if you have a big unexpected bill, you will have the resources to cover some if not all of it. Perhaps even more importantly, an emergency fund is psychologically significant. As you plan for your adoption, the constant flow of ordinary bills can begin to feel like an avalanche. If I'm unable to cover these basic responsibilities, you might think, how will I ever afford an adoption and provide for my baby after he or she is born? Controlling your spending to the point where you are able to save $1,000 will prove you are capable of great feats when you work in partnership with your spouse. Say no to trivial expenses and make wise tradeoffs that will put your family ahead.

Kicking debt to the curb is the next key to a foundation of financial security for your adoption. Let me be clear: I am not suggesting you need to be entirely debt-free before you adopt. Instead, I am telling you that your mindset needs to be clear and focused that debt is the enemy. Julie and I spent six years pushing our debt off the ledge. For about half of that time, we simply tried to make minimum payments and put a little extra toward the balance when we could. For the last half, we saw red, went crazy, and took extra jobs everywhere we could to remove financial insecurity from our lives once and for all.

Our adoption came toward the tail end of that final year. We realized our decision to adopt probably would postpone our ability to get rid of that last federal loan. At that point, though, we knew where we were headed. We weren't going to let an out-of-the-ordinary expense, particularly involving something as important as a new baby, derail what we had worked so hard to accomplish.

Remember where you've been when your financial path gets tough. Dave Ramsey frequently talks about the importance of getting out of debt with a bigger shovel, which means finding more income to make the process go faster. I knew adoption would mean I couldn't cut back on the extra writing and editing jobs I had found anytime soon. I spent a lot of mornings at the kitchen table at 4 a.m. watching the pink-and-purple hues of the sun break across our rolling lawn. Meanwhile, I typed frantically in a race to complete freelance assignments and ensure I could make progress before our sons awoke for breakfast. By the time nighttime rolled around, Julie and I were normally back at the grind, checking off the next boxes on our list of assignments, me on my freelance and Julie on her teaching or her Ph.D. work in science education. When we finally had a few free minutes together at 10:30 or 11 at night, I frequently succumbed to the exhaustion of the day, nodding off while sitting in front of the TV and sapping away most of the joy of spending time with my wife without little people pulling at our pant legs.

Yet we wouldn't trade the experience for a moment. It

taught us the meaning of a hard day's work and reminded us that we never wanted to be in the position where we would have to worry about whether we'd be able to cover our bills again. We appreciate what we have and where we are today because of what we lacked back then.

Work with your agency or clinic to understand when you will need to make payments, and fit those requirements into your family's budget.

Some expenses will be minimal, such as routine doctor's visits. Other expenses will be more intensive, such as paying for your embryos to be shipped to your clinic or the thawing and transfer of the embryos themselves. Once you know which payments will be due when, you can back up the calendar (which you've already created thanks to what you learned earlier in this book) and determine savings deadlines for each adoption milestone. If you discover you won't have all of the money saved by a particular date, you might visit with your clinic about the possibility of setting up a temporary payment plan. Better yet, push pause on your adoption, save the full amount you need, and pay for it entirely so you can proceed. Otherwise, you will bring a pattern of payments back into your life, and the cycle of debt you're trying to escape will continue.

You might even find that your financial choices raise eyebrows in a good way. Fertility treatments and adoptions too often lead families down a path of financial risk. Families take out loans without hesitation because of the high stakes. After all, we're talking about saving children and ensuring they have a forever home.

Think about your choices before you act, though. What kind of an environment will you provide for your child if you take money you would normally put toward his or her college savings and instead use it toward a loan that collects interest each month? I completely understand the deep and complex emotions that feed into the adoption process. I've felt many of the same things. I simply want to encourage you to use rational judgment, consult your spouse, and consider all possible moral and legal options for increasing your income to fund your adoption rather than simply buying time until your next paycheck and your next installment of debt. You might not have everything you desire for your family from a financial perspective in the earliest stages, but you will all benefit in a big way in the long run.

You can help your family by creating a monthly budget, controlling your spending, and celebrating milestones along the way.

The most helpful things you can do for your family's finances are also the easiest, with a little practice. A monthly budget will help you set goals for how much you plan to spend on groceries, utilities, rent or mortgage, and so on. By checking your bank statement several times per month and comparing it to your budget, you'll quickly see whether any of your financial decisions need to be realigned.

The process of doing a monthly budget also allows you to find leaks. Our family is constantly fighting leaks because our children love to swim. The boys will tramp into the kitchen, tracking in water, cut grass, and dirt, to loudly proclaim to Julie that the plastic pool has a leak. Someone must quickly plug the hole before water streams over the side in a wasteful waterfall. Out to the yard Julie goes, armed with the patch and pursued by three sweaty, droplet-covered boys. In a similar way, your budget will help you see the tradeoffs you are making by spending money in one area when it might be needed in another, such as saving to hit a big adoption savings goal.

Remember to make the most of it whenever you hit those targets too. Have an impromptu pizza party at home, create a financial thermometer to hang on your fridge and mark up as you go, or simply hold a dance party with your spouse or children in the living room. There's nothing wrong with a little elation and euphoria when you've worked hard and made great progress.

Your commitment to a strong financial footing will provide your family with positive returns in a way no other investment can do.

This is because you are creating habits that will be nearly impossible to break as you move forward and as your baby arrives. Are you using credit cards? Cut them up. Are you dependent on a hope and a dream that somehow you'll scrape up the cash or obtain a loan big enough to cover your dream? Stop living in a fantasy and get creative to earn extra income.

The faster you can get traction on your goal by taking steps that will get you measurably closer to holding that precious baby in your arms, the better. Sit down with your spouse and have a serious conversation about the future. What are you hopes and dreams for your children? What decisions can you make today about your finances that will benefit them in the years ahead?

Here's an example you might have experienced too. One of our biggest goals for our children is that they'll be able to cash-flow their education after high school. It's OK if they don't choose to go to college too. More and more young people are participating in apprenticeships or signing contracts that enable them to get a degree and then pay back their education costs as a percentage of income over several years. Whatever our children do, our aim is to instill in them the same strong desire for education that our parents did, and to use the financial blessings we've been given to provide them an early advantage as they start their adult lives.

You might have that type of a goal in mind for your adopted child. Or it might be more practical. Often, the best things in life cost the least. Julie and I were elated when we finally had enough flexibility in our budget to go out to eat every now and then. Even today, we don't officially allocate more than $30 a month toward frivolous spending. (Candidly, we manage to find extra dollars in other sections of the budget in a pinch. Don't tell Dave Ramsey!)

Whatever your ideal bank statement looks like, don't hang all of your optimism exclusively on that big final number. Julie and I beamed with pride when Micah held his first $100 bill through savings and birthday gifts. He reveled in it not because he totally appreciates what a Benjamin Franklin can buy—on the contrary, he's extraordinarily frugal and says he wants to buy something worth $17. Instead, he understood how hard he had worked on his chores. He also knew that a little extra income would enable him to buy things that Titus, whose money seems to flow directly from his pocket to Dollar Tree, could not.

Fight with everything you've got for your future newborn. Remember that today's sacrifices are well worth tomorrow's joys. As Mark Twain reminded us at the start of this chapter, hurting for cash crimps our style in ways large and small. Your adoption will require some capital, but the little life you are bringing into the world is worth every penny.

Dust off your piggy bank and start collecting.

Discussion Questions

- How comfortable are you and your spouse with your finances as they stand today? If you aren't completely satisfied, what do you wish were different? (If you are completely satisfied, keep up the good work.)

- What are two or three concrete steps you can take to ensure you will have the cash to fund your adoption? Options could include taking on a side job, cutting back expenses in your budget, or setting individual savings goals to match your adoption time line.

- What blessings will your baby enjoy because of the hard work and sacrifices you have made in the area of finances?

8

ACCLIMATE YOUR DARLINGS

There are no secrets that time does not reveal.

—JEAN RACINE

In this chapter, you will learn

- How you can foster a special relationship with your pre-born baby even while acknowledging and celebrating her special conception story

- Why you should publicly and frequently talk about your baby's adoption with your family, friends, and others in your life

- How to exercise sensitivity in your conversations about adoption, particularly with children already in your family and with those who might be skeptical about the process

I revealed our adoption in an otherwise ordinary Sunday sermon this past fall. To be honest, I didn't know what the reaction would be. But I had a message to deliver on the value of human life, on the strong biblical case for adoption, and on our own journey of adoption that Julie and I wanted our fellow church members to know about.

The response proved more positive than I could have imagined. Friends gave us hugs and had tears in their eyes. One shared that she had always dreamed of adoption early in her marriage and had never had the opportunity to pursue it.

I don't know about your church, but mine is a small country congregation. We're on a state highway, so it's not out in the sticks, but topics such as embryo adoption aren't everyday fare. It's impossible to get a read on what everyone thought, nor is it any of my business. Everyone already knew Julie was expecting, but only a handful knew the special story of the baby growing in her uterus.

You didn't buy this book to learn how to give a really shocking pulpit-buster, though. You want to know how in the world this chapter will help you in your adoption.

Because you are adopting, you are volunteering to explain your decision to others.

Ultimately, you are practicing to explain this story to your new baby as he or she grows up. The way you tell the story will become more detailed with time, but the core elements will remain the same.

This illustrates the importance of beginning this process within the four walls of your home. If you and your spouse are the only people presently living in your household, you can skip this section. But if you have other family residing with you, including children, it's important to begin the adoption conversation early and often. In our family, we began this process months before Julie's embryo transfer. Part of our agency's home-study process involved family interviews, and this included our caseworker interviewing our children about themselves and their feelings about having a new baby in the family. To avoid catching them off guard, we chose to explain some of the essential details of our plans.

It's never a good idea to force the issue at an awkward time, nor is it a good idea to incessantly bring up the fact Phoebe is adopted. The purpose of having the conversation at all is to normalize Phoebe's story. Her life is just as important to us as any of her siblings, even though her conception and arrival in Julie's uterus might have been different than the boys'. We've explained that in her case, her placing family's sperm and egg came together in a doctor's office, whereas that process happened inside Julie with the boys. With all four of our children, the outcome was the same: our babies grew in Mommy's tummy until it was time for them to be born. You can imagine how intriguing this is to little minds under the age of ten.

There are always plenty of questions, but the end result is always a twinkle in their eyes, Micah's in particular as the oldest and ablest to understand what we're describing, and greater admiration for their little sister and her placing family. Together, we have fostered our love for Phoebe by fully appreciating where she came from and the precious gift God gave us. You can replicate this in your own family, and I recommend doing so in the way that makes sense for you. As your child grows older, you should add new age-appropriate details so he or she knows the adoption story.

Families didn't always bring information like this out into the open, and the consequences have been devastating. If you've ever read stories of siblings who mistakenly discovered each other through DNA-testing websites or media interviews, you know how heart-wrenching this must be. In the past, children were placed with families with next to no information about their genetic families, prompting generations of children to long desperately for more details about their origins and to spend countless hours searching for those relatives. The adoption community largely has shifted to a much more open model in which the placing family and the adoptive family mutually decide the degree of openness they desire. In some cases, it might be exchanging the occasional snail-mail letter and photos. In other cases, such as ours, it might involve social media posts, text messages, and in-person family get-togethers. Whatever you do, even in closed or anonymous adoptions, seek out the best possible life for your child.

Part of acclimating the people in your life to the idea of adoption involves answering difficult questions, but you should never shy away from talking about the subject.

Your child's identity should in no way solely be defined by adoption. At the same time, you shouldn't seek to scrub his or her history of adoption because that will always be a fundamental part of his or her reality. Your child will always have two families, adoptive and placing, that will define him or her. Without question, you and your spouse are the parents, and your love knows no bounds. But with embryo adoption, in many cases, there is another couple in the world who also loves your child deeply, even though the relationship might be very different from your own.

You can think of yourself as an ambassador. Suppose the president of the United States calls you up and explains her decision (yes, in my dream future, a woman is president—I'm now father to a daughter, after all) to appoint you to the position of ambassador to another country. You will become the face of the United States to the people who live there, ensuring our nations live at peace with each other, and helping to serve the interests of both countries in whatever ways that you can. The art of diplomacy is having the moral courage to speak your mind with gentleness and to look out for the best interests of others.

This applies directly to adoption. You will hear all kinds of comments, ideas, and thoughts on the subject. In some cases—and this has been true for me on more than one occasion—you might only get an icy silence. Don't read too much into the comments people make. People who genuinely love you and your family are going to have an implicit degree of trust in your decision to adopt, even if they don't fully understand it. As an adoption ambassador, it's your job to explain your decisions in plain, easy-to-comprehend terms. You don't need to be a doctor or a scientist, nor do you need to apologize if you don't have all the answers. Adoption is deeply personal and fully coaching someone through the thought processes and complex decision tree you and your spouse followed isn't necessary. You owe it to your child to validate his or her life as much as anyone else. You also owe it to him or her to keep your conversations professional and without the drama some who seek to test you are seeking.

The ability to interpret the words and body language of those around you will help you exercise sensitivity in your conversations about adoption.

I'm notoriously bad about confronting difficult issues over email. Next to simply grabbing a backpack and vanishing into the woods without a trace, email is perhaps the worst method for dealing with difficult subjects. Nonetheless, an email is what I chose to use to introduce my parents to the fact Julie and I were pursuing embryo adoption.

In true Nate character, the email ended up being perhaps 8,000 words long, included links to information on embryo adoption and attempted to messily explain our decision without sounding as if I had joined a baby cult. My parents adore Phoebe and supported us fully through the process, but it quickly became clear that I had some explaining to do, as Desi Arnaz used to tell Lucille Ball. Perhaps the most obvious question involved why we had chosen to adopt when we already had three healthy biological sons of our own.

This question is so common that I ended up writing a blog post titled "Why Couples Without Infertility Adopt Embryos" that mirrored at least some of what I shared with my mom and dad at the time. The five reasons are:

1. Friends of friends had successfully adopted embryos and brought them to term.

2. Julie's background is as a scientist studying infertility, specifically endometriosis.

3. We had discussed adoption since before we were married ten years ago.

4. As Christians, we believe life begins at conception, and that every embryo deserves the best chance at life.

5. Embryo adoption is about half as expensive as other forms of adoption.

At no point did those reasons have to make sense to my parents, or to anyone else for that matter. My goal simply was to let them know of our decision because they are some of the most important people in our lives. The same was true for Julie's family, where her mom quickly understood and appreciated our decision because of her own experiences with infertility.

The choice to adopt embryos is basically the opposite of staging a second mission to the moon. Instead of doing something big and bold that will be plastered across the nightly news and social media, you are doing something microscopic that carries a tremendous amount of risk with a sliver of hope that you'll get to meet a chubby little face in the end.

That doesn't make your mission any less important, nor does it remove your responsibility to talk about it, normalize it, and be open about it. You never know: that little embryo might end up staging the moon mission after all.

Discussion Questions

- Think of three people in your life with whom you'd like to share your decision to adopt embryos. How will you initiate the conversation? How will you explain your choice?

- How do you prefer to communicate with others (e.g., in person, text, social media, email, phone)? How can you use these to share your family's story with loved ones at the right time, in a way that respect's your family's privacy?

- What steps will you take to protect your child and your family in cases where it isn't appropriate to discuss adoption in depth or at all? Think of a simple phrase you can use to end a conversation or change the topic.

9

CONNECT WITH YOUR BEST PLACING FAMILY

You don't choose your family. They are God's gift to you, as you are to them.

—DESMOND TUTU

In this chapter, you will learn

- Why matching with the right family can be among the most exciting and nerve-wracking parts of the embryo adoption process
- How to avoid discouragement if your match falls through
- Why you should jump into a time machine to imagine your embryo baby's future relationship with these two important families

There is a special place in my heart for UFOs. I'm not quite to the "attends all conferences on extraterrestrials within a 200-mile radius" on the crazy spectrum, but I'm not that far off either. If you've ever seen a science-fiction movie, you've probably encountered the trope about time—it never seems to apply to people from beyond the stars. As the story often goes, those whose technology exceeds our understanding are able to zoom from one place to another in the snap of your fingers. This side of Hollywood, people who claim they've been abducted by aliens often describe what's known as missing time. One minute they see the bright lights of a foreign spacecraft, the next minute they were sitting in their car. Somehow, three hours have elapsed.

This experience is similar to what you might encounter on the road to your placing family. No, adoption agencies and clinics aren't storing embryos for E.T., at least as far as I can tell. But when you reach the matching phase of your adoption experience, time truly seems to speed up. It also gets a lot more real. Before, you and your spouse essentially operated a 24/7 call center, medical clinic, and PR agency. You've answered lots of questions, taken plenty of medical tests, and given your best embryo adoption explanation speech to countless inquirers.

Those requirements are important, and those relationships are essential. What you'll do with your placing family is on a completely different level, though. If you've paid attention up to this point, you know that most embryo adoptions are open to some degree. You probably have connected the dots and discovered that means your placing family will hold a special place in your own family for the remainder of your life. In many senses, you are not only adopting embryos, but you are also adopting an entirely new branch into your family tree. Your embryo baby's placing family will graft you into its own family as well.

I don't mean to scare you here, but this is serious stuff. You've already committed to adoption. If you've been following my recommendations, you're well on your way to saving the necessary funds for the process, and you've begun normalizing your family to embryo adoption.

Your placing journey moves you beyond the idea of adoption and helps you turn your adoption dreams into reality.

If this stage goes according to plan, you will soon be within one degree of separation from your embryo baby. You'll soon get to see what your placing family looks like. You'll be able to imagine what your child or children might look like. You'll be able to thank God in your prayers for this beautiful gift you are receiving and name the placing family who made it possible.

First, however, you've got some work to do. In chapter 5, we discussed creating a family profile to help potential matching families get to know you better. Julie and I included everything from photos of our parents and special friends to descriptions of how we met, why we chose to adopt, and what type of relationship we would like to have with our placing family. From the very beginning, we knew we wanted to maintain an extremely open relationship, within the comfort level of our placing family. After all, we had our own children, and we could imagine how much we'd want to remain in touch with our biological babies if anyone were to adopt from us.

If you are working with an agency, they will help you through this process. Ask for templates if they are available, or search online for examples. Remember that everything you compile for your placing family, from your profile to your medical records, should be completely transparent. You don't necessarily need to spend five pages discussing that one black-sheep relative who ended up in jail three times. At the same time, it's especially meaningful for your placing family to have confidence in you and your spouse, your relationship with each other and any existing children, your connection to grandparents and other extended family, etc. If you are a Christian family and expect it's highly likely your placing family will be Christians as well, make sure your faith shines through. After all, Jesus condemned people who loudly boasted about their faith from street corners yet purely did so for attention. Instead, make it clear from the examples you share that your family puts God at the center of its home, that you regularly attend worship services, and that you engage in wholesome activities as a family to grow closer to one another and those in your community. Your placing family is entrusting with you their embryos, and those embryos are unique human lives. Help them have peace of mind their decision, which they've likely prayed over for months if not years, is the right one.

Once you've completed the family profile and other materials for your agency, and you've finished your home study, you'll need to get your patience on.

If you are working with an agency, its staff will begin the process of outreach to families with embryos. They will have the first right of refusal. Your agency will alert you when your information has been shared with a family, and the family will have several weeks to review your materials, pray about their decision, and let your agency know of their decision. (If you are working directly with a clinic, keep in mind many of these steps might not be required.)

At this point, you will probably feel a mix of euphoria and terror. The excitement and joy you feel may stem from the fact you've poured your heart and soul out to your agency, and they are going to be an ambassador on your behalf. Their job isn't to convince a placing family that you're the one. It's simply to study and know your family inside and out, and then to match you with a family they think is a really good fit because of the similar values and backgrounds you share.

The fear you feel stems from the unknown. I don't know about you, but I don't handle rejection particularly well. I've gotten better because as a journalist, if you aren't able to withstand near-constant editing, feedback, reworking, and reinventing, you won't stick around in the newsroom. You'll go find a job building widgets where the process stays the same and the fear of rejection rarely looms. The corollary is that as a would-be adoptive parent, you face the real possibility of rejection.

I've explained before that Julie and I knew our risk of rejection would be a bit higher than for other couples because of our biological children. Many couples with remaining embryos seek to place them with families who, like them, have faced infertility. Yet going through the adoption process and successfully checking off each step has a way of boosting your confidence. We thought we were ready for anything, but in actuality, that initial rejection caught us off guard.

It all happened over email. (This seems to be a theme for my life.) One day, we opened our inboxes and found a note from our agency explaining they had shared our information with a possible placing family. This happened around the winter holidays, so we knew timing could be a bit touch and go. We were thrilled. At last! We knew our time had come, and we waited on pins and needles to hear this family's decision. After a few weeks of radio silence, I checked in with our agency. They had requested some additional information from the genetic family on their preferences and appreciated our patience. They reminded us adoption could be a lengthy process. I thanked our agency for their help and hard work and returned to waiting mode.

Then came the follow-up. The family our agency had selected by carefully matching our interests and backgrounds had chosen not to place their embryos with us. If you encounter something similar, I will warn you this can feel devastating. You begin questioning what might have been wrong with the information you shared and which factors might have led to the family's decision.

Don't let an experience like this derail your hope. Keep in mind there are dozens of possible factors influencing each family's decision. Some are very practical and deeply held, such as the desire to help couples facing infertility have a child. I wouldn't be a bit surprised if this factor played a role in our initial rejection, but the truth is we'll never know. It is a private decision, and every family deserves to have their wishes respected. We would request the same.

Yes, rejection will inevitably delay your adoption time line, but any agency worth its salt will warn you of this possibility early and often. Ours did. In the world of business, failing to make a deal means you're one step closer to closing your next deal. In the case of adoption, one mismatch with a placing family is simply God's way of aligning your journey in the right direction. The next match your agency or clinic makes might be exactly what is meant for you.

On match day, you will feel like a million bucks.

Our good news arrived in February 2017, when our agency contacted us to let us know that the second couple with whom we had been matched, John and Kris, had decided to place their embryos with us. They had three embryos, and we had up to two weeks to review their family profile, medical history, and other details. We needed to spend time on our decision but also couldn't dawdle because this placing family deserved a home for its embryos. If Julie and I weren't the right people, another couple might be. I quickly responded that we were elated and would use the time wisely to get to a decision quickly.

Your heart will be pounding in your chest as you pull up your possible placing family's letter. Of course, the letter they wrote—and the one we wrote for them—were written in a generic "Dear Adoptive Family" style. But there's no mistaking that when you find the right family, you will know that letter is meant especially for you. I immediately fell in love with our placing family. I studied the story of their dating days and marriage, the joyous welcome of their oldest daughter, their subsequent tragic losses through miscarriage, and finally their decision to pursue IVF.

I found it incredible that this couple's love for their children extended not only to their three existing children but also to their three remaining embryos. Some families might have destroyed them, authorized them to be sent to a lab for research, or simply kept them in below-freezing conditions. In our case, our placing family felt the urgency of giving their embryos—frozen in 2008 just months after Julie and I were married—the best chance possible at a great life. There are few times in life when you feel like recreating one of those epic movie scenes where the main character falls to his knees, bowed low by the magnitude of the situation he's facing. For me, this was one of those moments.

But you might appreciate hearing from our actual placing family because it's their decision that led us to this point.

After reading an early version of this chapter, Kris shared

the following narrative of their experience. I think you'll quickly see just how much they love their babies—and you'll better appreciate the many emotional stages of the placement process. I hope her and John's story, included in italics on the following pages, will inspire you as much as it has inspired me:

Our journey began in 2002 when John and I were married. In 2003, our daughter Kassidy was born. We got pregnant easily and had an easy pregnancy.

In 2005, I miscarried twins around 11 to 12 weeks into the pregnancy, after we heard heartbeats. Then in 2006, I miscarried one baby, again around 11 to 12 weeks into the pregnancy, and also after we heard the heartbeat.

Later in 2006, I went through several rounds of intrauterine insemination (IUI), all of which were unsuccessful.

In 2007, my doctor ran tests and found that I have methylene tetrahydrofolate reductase (MTHFR), a genetic condition that can contribute to infertility.

The next year, I started the IVF process with Dr. Peter Ahlering. In 2008, the first round of IVF was unsuccessful. The second round of IVF, also in 2008, was successful. I was hyperstimulated and produced 18 eggs. Most were fertilized, and my doctor kept the six healthiest embryos, implanted three in me, and froze the remaining embryos. Our twins, Kallie and Kaiden, arrived in 2009.

John and I immediately knew we did not want to destroy the embryos, donate them to science, or give them to an agency to donate. We knew we wanted an open adoption, and we were open to as much contact as the adopting family desired. (We were thrilled to find out how close Julie and Nate lived!)

I started to call Snowflakes® when the twins were about one year old. But every time I called, I would start crying, and I knew I wasn't ready to let go of them. I would think I was ready and would call—only to break down again. I felt like I was failing as a mom to the embryos left behind. It was a gradual process of letting go of the feelings I had— abandonment, guilt, loss—and letting God take control. It was when I gave it to Him that it all became easy and, finally, exciting.

We always planned to bless a family who had struggled with infertility, but when Julie and Nate's family profile came up, I felt peace and God's voice saying, This is your family. It became an easy decision when we read their history and saw their pictures. We knew that our son Kaiden would be right at home with their boys. We also made our decision to give our precious embryos the best chance of survival. Julie's body knew what do with Phoebe, even as an embryo. The same may not have been true for other families that struggle with infertility.

We are beyond blessed and so excited that our families will forever be bonded together. We look forward to a lifetime of love and laughter!

Just as our placing family went through several extremely important stages, you, too, will you go through multiple— admittedly very different—stages to reach a decision on your placing family.

Your decision won't begin and end solely with your own opinion either. I highly recommend you take several additional steps. First, pray about it. Second, sleep on it. I don't advocate making life-changing decisions on an empty stomach, either, but definitely pray and sleep before acting. You'll also want to involve your fertility clinic because they might have some additional questions. In our case, they wanted to see

- legal documentation stating the embryos were ours, once our contract had been signed;

- infectious disease testing on the embryos' biological parents, along with the dates on which they were created and any additional testing the agency might have requested; and

- an embryology log with more details on the quality and history of each embryo.

Remember that adoption is a process that requires all kinds of experts working in different time frames and often in different geographies. This is your next chance to take the lessons you learned in chapter 6 about being your best advocate and put them to work. With a few quick and polite emails or phone calls, you can make sure everyone is on the same page about where you are in the matching process and who needs to know what to give your prospective placing family a big yes.

It's worth noting that whether you work with an agency or a clinic, your final match will feel a bit like dating with a chaperone.

Your agency or clinic has expertise in helping families navigate the embryo adoption and transfer process. It's too soon to interact directly with your placing family, but you can begin to work out those details once you've alerted your agency that you are ready to move forward with adoption of the embryos. The next step will be to complete your contract with your placing family and to have it notarized. Among other details of the contract is information about how often and in what ways you will communicate with your placing family. For example, our contract specified that we would alert our placing family to our baby's birth soon after the event as well as details about the baby's health, weight, height, and name. We also committed to regular yearly check-ins with our family until our baby reaches adulthood.

You should view your contract as the bare minimum responsibility you have to your baby and her placing family. In our case, we were overjoyed to make the connection with our family because we had longed for this day. We couldn't believe we had been blessed to be matched with a family that viewed these embryos in the same way we did. We were excited to build our family in a way we had never fully imagined and in partnership with an entirely new family who would remain incredibly special despite the absence of any blood relation. By the time we welcomed Phoebe into the world, we had already begun exchanging emails, text messages, and new family photos with our placing family. John and Kris and their children had become an integral part of our lives, and they had welcomed us into their family with open arms too.

Our agency gladly took off the training wheels when all of the necessary legal paperwork was in place, and it continues to be an important part of our adoption story. In the weeks after Phoebe's birth, they reached out to remind us that part of our contract stated we would write a thank-you letter to our placing family and share some photos of the baby. We did just this, and it provided a wonderful touchpoint to further express our gratitude before we met for the first time in person.

Yes, you can meet your placing family face-to-face, and it can be the start of an amazing relationship.

We did exactly this, and it happened in the most surprising way we could have expected. As we began connecting with our placing family through our agency, Julie and I assumed they must live far away. Kimberly, the director of the embryo adoption program at our agency whom you met in chapter 2, once told me a majority of embryo adoptions happen across state lines. Families don't have the luxury of seeing each other in person often, so written correspondence and photos have to do.

Well, Birts break rules, and our adoption proved to be no exception. Rather than matching with a couple stationed in the outskirts of Maine, we had matched with a couple just 90 minutes away from our home. They live in the town where Julie grew up, right near her parents, grandparents, and extended family. Some might call that a lucky break. We had no problem calling it what it is: providence.

We knew the proximity of our placing family would enable us to introduce in person the little girl they had helped us bring into the world. We just didn't know quite how it would happen.

Thankfully, our placing family took care of that for us. It's my hope that you will find a special way to meet your placing family too. We went back and forth for weeks by text message, trying to find a date when our busy calendars would align. Finally, we discovered we would both be in St. Louis on a certain Sunday afternoon. John and Kris and their family invited us to join them for a barbecue, and they also told us how much they and their children wanted to give Phoebe several special gifts.

We arrived at their house on a sunny, warm afternoon and parked in the steep driveway. As we began to unload the children, Kris, her sister, and some of Phoebe's biological siblings came outside to greet us. They radiated pure warmth, welcoming us into their home and introducing us not only to John and the other children but also to Kris' father. We sat in their living room, recounting one another's feelings and thoughts through each stage of the adoption process. The family took turns holding Phoebe, admiring her tiny fingers and toes and that coy little grin.

Kris took the boys outside to go swimming while Julie and I visited with Kris on the porch and John brought us something cold to drink. Pretty soon, all of us were gathered in the backyard, recounting stories from our lives back home and our family heritages. John barbecued a tremendous spread of hamburgers, bratwursts, and sausages, and others had prepared potato salad and a whole lot of other side dishes. We took the party inside and continued the conversation.

Phoebe lay on a blanket in the living room as our children and Kris and John's took turns playing with her. On the one hand, we all were getting to know one another for the first time. On the other, it was as if we were picking up midconversation, having been brought together by invisible forces we had never fully appreciated until that moment.

What we had thought might last two hours extended to five. After dinner, we reconvened in the living room for gifts. There were pink bags, boxes, and cards with heartfelt messages sharing with Phoebe how much her placing family loved her and had looked forward to meeting her. Julie and I cherish those notes and will keep them in a memory book where our daughter can refer to them often as she grows up.

Perhaps the most incredible token they gifted Phoebe that day is a pink satin blanket with a rabbit sewn onto one corner. It's a blanket her genetic sister cherished as a child—the same sister who came from the IVF round in which Phoebe was formed. Her genetic sister even coined a word for her special relationship with Phoebe. She calls our daughter her *friendster*, a nod to the fact that while they didn't grow up together, they will always share a deep connection.

After packing up the children and preparing to return to Julie's parents, we stopped to admire baby photos of Phoebe's IVF buddies—her twin biological sister and brother—as babies. Kris and John shared how each baby had acted growing up, and they revealed another detail we hadn't known. The doctor who had helped Kris with her IVF cycle is the same doctor whose clinic Julie had used to bring Phoebe to term.

I can't help but think about all of the people whose decisions had a direct impact on my daughter's life. If one person had chosen to go in a slightly different direction, we might never have met Phoebe. And yet, here we are.

As you prepare for your own matching journey, I hope our story will give you the hope you need to embrace the joy of the moment. Your baby is inherently special. His or her life will only be enhanced by the incredible placing family who made the decision to save your baby's life.

Cherish them always.

Discussion Questions

- What kind of a relationship do you wish to foster with your placing family? Discuss with your spouse the degree of openness that will make the most sense initially, keeping in mind you can always make adjustments as time goes on.

- Which factors about your prospective placing family will be most important to you as you evaluate whether to adopt their embryos? Which unique aspects of your family do you hope will be most influential in your placing family's decision to place embryos with you?

- When in the development of your relationship with your placing family might you entertain the idea of meeting in person? Discuss with your spouse what you hope that first get-together might look like.

PART IV:
THE TRANSFER

10

TINY LOSSES

Grief is in two parts. The first is loss.
The second is the remaking of life.

—ANNE ROIPHE

In this chapter, you will learn

- How to prepare yourself for the possibility not all of your frozen embryos will survive the thaw

- Why it is important to understand what happens to each of your embryos for the sake of closure, and how to obtain the information you need from your fertility clinic

- How to communicate news of lost embryos to your placing family in a sensitive and understanding way, and how to grieve any embryos that are not viable

I experienced the acute pain of death for the first time at the funeral of my maternal grandfather, James King. I was thirty-one. The in-town service had ended, and we had wound our way through the countryside to the small cemetery on my grandparents' farm in Middle Tennessee. The November afternoon couldn't have been more spectacular. Golden leaves fell gently from the trees and wove their way slowly to the ground. My cousin-in-law played the violin. My uncle said a few words in tribute to my grandfather. A longtime family friend delivered a prayer through a tear-stained, broken voice. I led our gathering in a hymn. As we said our goodbyes and the staff from the funeral home lowered my grandfather's casket into the ground, the sense of finality loomed large. We filled the hours that followed with laughter, shared memories, and good food, but none of it could remove the nagging sense of a light that had gone out of our lives and for which an adequate substitute would never be found.

You have undoubtedly experienced the loss of dear family members or friends as well. The pain can be excruciating, and it can be difficult to know how to move forward without them. In this chapter, I want to help you understand a very different kind of loss. Just as the loss of someone we have known for decades affects each of us differently, so, too, does the loss of a tiny embryo you might only have known on paper, through correspondence with your placing family. What is lost is tiny, but the loss is not tiny.

One of the risks of embryo adoption is that not all of the embryos you plan to bring to term will survive the process of thawing. Yet do a quick Google search, and you'll discover fertility clinics that boast of incredible success rates on the order of 95 percent. It's true the technology to thaw embryos has improved with every passing year. In our case, our embryos were close to a decade old at the time of thawing and transfer. We had two embryos frozen on day 6 of development and one on day 5. The day 5 embryo had developed faster, while the day 6 embryos had been slower, suggesting the best chances of success rested with the faster-growing embryo. Nonetheless, we had every intention of bringing each embryo to term at the right time. Julie's doctor had advised he would be comfortable with us transferring two embryos to start. We would save the last embryo for a future transfer.

During your adoption, you will probably discover that most couples place multiple embryos with adoptive couples rather than placing a single embryo. You should discuss with your spouse and your doctor how to approach the thawing process in light of the risks, on the one hand, and the possibility of carrying multiples, on the other. Once you make the decision and have communicated it to your fertility clinic, the timing of medicines and the transfer itself (see chapter 11) will be orchestrated carefully to ensure the best chance of success for all embryos.

I will let Julie describe what happened in our case, as she wrote a guest post for my blog titled "July 11: A Day Of Joy And Of Sorrow," that encapsulates our embryo loss experience better than I ever could have:

> Exactly one year ago today, after many shots, pills, and privacy probing doctor's appointments, we had finally arrived at embryo transfer day. I was so nervous on this day and hormonal! We had planned to have the embryologist thaw out two of the three embryos we had adopted for transfer. After I had gotten changed in the prep room into a hospital gown for the transfer, our coordinator brought us back a photo of the embryo that was ready to transfer. I remember looking at Nate in awe at the little ball of cells—our baby. Then the questions started forming in mind: What about the other one? What had happened?
>
> When our coordinator returned, we asked and she offhandedly replied that the other embryo hadn't

survived the thaw. While she said it so commonly, it hit me hard. Later, we would talk to the embryologist and find out that in all, two of the embryos thawed did not survive. There were no other embryos remaining. While we had prepared ourselves mentally that they might not all survive the thaw process, I had inwardly hoped that our little babies would all defy the statistics and get a chance to grow into three little newborns.

When we found out that we had been matched with three embryos, Nate and I had many conversations about how we would handle three more kids. He even priced conversion vans to haul all of them around. You see, we believe that every embryo is a person, and we were actively planning, physically and mentally, to have each of those three precious babies join our family.

I still think of those two babies daily who did not get the chance to be tickled by three little brothers. They never got the chance to laugh and giggle with their daddy. They never got the chance to snuggle with me through late-night nursing sessions. I might not have had the opportunity to grow them or shelter them in my body, but I still love them dearly.

While the adoption process was filled with sadness of lost embryos, physical pain, and emotional turmoil, I would do it again in an instant. Having that peace that all was made well and that none of these three souls are sitting frozen in a liquid nitrogen tank makes it worth every sacrifice. The smiles and laughter of our sweet daughter, Phoebe, are just an additional joy that cements my belief that every baby (or embryo) is a unique and important life to be protected and cherished.

As heart-wrenching as it might be to broach the subject with your fertility clinic, you and your placing family deserve to know what happens to all embryos you adopt.

That might require a little investigation. In our case, the timing of our initial questioning unfortunately coincided with our transfer date. We had signed a contract stating that we wanted our clinic to thaw and transfer two embryos. But upon seeing the snapshot of the single embryo, we were alternately delighted and terrified. What had happened to the other embryo, and why hadn't our clinic alerted us sooner if something had gone wrong? My brain tends to jump to the worst-case scenario, and yours is probably no different.

We didn't get a straight answer that day. But in retrospect I attribute the miscommunication largely to the fact that clinics coordinate their transfers for many families on the same day, creating a busy atmosphere where details are easy to overlook. I spent the next few days placing phone calls and emails to our agency. To the credit of Julie's fertility doctor, she quickly put us in touch with our embryologist, who explained what had happened. The embryologist explained that the clinic's primary focus is to secure a viable pregnancy for each of its patients. When a thawed embryo is deemed inviable, the clinic thaws the next available embryo for the transfer process.

In our case, the day 6 embryos—the ones that had developed more slowly—were thawed first and did not survive, so the embryologist successfully thawed the day 5 embryo next. He provided this detailed explanation via email and offered to answer additional questions as they occurred to us.

Nothing can prepare you to receive this kind of news. True, the relationship you've fostered with your embryos will be very different from relationships with longtime friends and family. Yet those of us who view the world through Christian eyes know embryos aren't merely a clump of cells. They are human, and they have souls, as do fully born children. It follows that we will one day meet these little people in heaven, a truly mind-bending thought that can amplify the sense of loss.

I encourage you to spend time alone with your spouse and with your private thoughts if you experience the loss of embryos during your adoption journey. To the outside world, grieving an embryo might sound ridiculous. But I can assure you there are other adoptive families who have experienced what you are feeling and can empathize with the loss, whether it feels large or small at the time.

Once you have grieved, you are prepared to deliver the news to your placing family.

Because we had begun corresponding with our placing family by email, we could quickly get in touch. I remember the sinking feeling in the pit of my stomach as I crafted a note to our placing family. Weeks earlier, we had explained our intention to transfer two embryos. Yet now we had changed our tune, against our wishes, and were going to correct the record to state that Julie's doctor had only transferred a single embryo and that the others had not survived. Mercifully, our placing family reacted with sorrow and understanding.

In the months after you transfer, you might discover you have new opportunities to share the full story with your placing family. Ours had more questions about exactly what had transpired to lead to a single viable embryo, so Julie and I took turns explaining our experience from beginning to end. We made a point of reiterating that we had similarly felt a tremendous sense of loss, and we conveyed how our wishes had been to bring all three embryos to term. That conversation brought an additional sense of closure even though all of us had hoped the outcome would be different.

Life will never be a perfect mirror of what we hoped it

would be. Sadly, some adoptive families find that none of the embryos they have adopted are viable. They must begin the matching process over again, compounding the grief of the experience. In our case, our single embryo developed beautifully into our daughter, Phoebe.

Whatever your experience, know that the emotions you are feeling, and any losses you face, are entirely valid. Take the time you need to grieve and process these events before you move on.

When you are ready to continue to the next chapter, I will prepare you for the joy that awaits when your embryo baby is finally a part of your family.

Discussion Questions

- How are you preparing yourself for the possibility one or more of your adopted embryos will not survive the thaw? Whom will you and your spouse lean on for support?

- What is the most comfortable way for you to communicate questions and concerns to your fertility clinic about the thawing and transfer process? What questions will you ask to ensure you have closure about the fate of your embryos?

- How will you communicate the story of your embryos to your placing family? How can you demonstrate sensitivity to their needs and convey your shared sense of loss?

11

THE TRIUMPHANT EMBRYO

Tough times never last, but tough people do.

—Robert H. Schuller

In this chapter, you will learn

- How doctors help adoptive moms prepare to receive a newly thawed embryo through appointments, medication, and the shipping of the embryo itself

- How adoptive dads can provide the best possible support before, during, and after a frozen embryo transfer

- What happens during the frozen embryo transfer itself, what recovery looks like, and how quickly you will know whether your embryo has successfully survived the process and implanted

Sometimes, you have to go small to go big. I made this discovery when my parents decided to remodel their basement with three walls of built-in bookcases.

Most Colorado families probably have skis and snowboards tucked away under the stairs, or beautiful oil paintings of mountain vistas, or old-fashioned pioneer wagon wheels. My dad kept floor-to-ceiling shelves of books. No one has more eclectic tastes than my dad, and in perhaps the greatest irony of his career, this born-again librarian—a convert from computer programming—affirmed regularly his belief that the best book is a bought book. He even has an intricate cataloging system separating history from sci-fi, classics from world religions, medical guidebooks from mathematics texts.

As kids, my siblings and I loved this because it meant our own libraries were (and remain) well supplied. But the remodeling exercise revealed an important truth about books: to stack them onto newly constructed shelves, you must first unstack them, one by one, off the old shelves. And because none of us has been granted access to the catalog by which the books are kept, we deferred to Dad to make sure everything went back into its proper place.

We needed a guide who could hold the metaphorical torch and light the path ahead. Dad had a vision for our little basement, and the result proved stunning: handcrafted wooden bookcases that continue to hold thousands of my dad's most treasured possessions.

Just as the basement library exercise proved a success, so, too, can your embryo transfer journey be successful. But you will need a guide, and in the world of fertility clinics, that guide is known as a third-party coordinator.

A good coordinator will ease your fears about the momentous transfer process and teach you exactly what you need to do to create the best physical environment for your adopted embryos.

The start of the embryo transfer process began for us about two and a half months before our actual transfer date. It looked something like this, and yours probably will too:

1) Julie visited her fertility doctor about a month and a half before the transfer for a fluid ultrasound. The process ensured the doctor wouldn't need to do any surgical procedures to remove items such as uterine polyps or fibroids that could hurt the chances of success.

2) She began taking a birth control pill to ensure her body would be ready to receive the embryo at the same time as other clinic patients. Clinics tend to batch transfers into a single day or over a few tightly monitored days because of the staff and specialized instruments needed for the procedures. (Other clinics may recommend natural monitoring of the mother's menstrual cycle to avoid the use of birth control medicine.)

3) Our clinic provided us with a calendar of dates on which to take or stop taking certain medications. The calendar also included important appointment dates, the transfer date itself, and other important information for her to remember.

Your coordinator will coach you through the complexities of this process. I'm thankful my wife's background is in reproductive medicine, so she knew what to expect and could explain it to me. That didn't stop me from badgering our coordinator by email and not a few times by phone for more information or to clarify comments the doctor had made to Julie during appointments I hadn't attended.

Our clinic ended up being about 90 minutes from our home, so this phase of the adoption journey proved especially taxing on Julie. Sometimes it seemed as if Julie needed to travel back and forth weekly to ensure everything with her body had been going according to plan.

The medications aren't always oral, and pain is a necessary part of the process.

If you are a husband reading this book, I want to assure you that you are still a man even if you are unwilling to stick your wife in the buttocks with a needle. I openly committed to Julie on several occasions that I would be happy to help with this part of the process, which she had to do daily for several weeks in a row.

I changed my tune after I saw the size of the needle. I didn't know you could inject your body with crochet hooks and live to tell about it.

Julie took it all in stride and simply kept her medicine in an upper cabinet in the bathroom where the children couldn't reach it. She even let the boys watch a few times, which prompted all kinds of questions and body humor. Very literally, Julie had committed to doing anything for this embryo baby.

You and your spouse will find endurance to be an incredible asset on your adoption journey. When our family took a trip back west to visit my family for the Fourth of July holiday, just a week before the transfer, Julie loaded up her medications and faithfully took all of them. I don't know about you, but sticking myself with needles when I'm supposed to be having a bit of a getaway doesn't sound like the best time in the world. See your present circumstances as part of a bigger picture that will completely change your life for the better, and view them for what they are—temporary.

How can husbands support the process? You can help by

heaping praise upon your wife, offering prayers on her behalf, asking how she is feeling, and inquiring how you can be helpful. Those are honestly the best solutions I've found. You can't live the experience for her, and it does you no good to furrow your brow or moan and groan over how sorry you feel that she has to go through all of this. Assuming you are on the same page, you are both glad your wife is going through this stage to bring your baby into the world. You can furrow your brow all you like, but it will probably drive your wife crazy. Be there for her, step in to help with the kids when she isn't feeling well or is otherwise unavailable, and remember to take actions to show you care.

When the time is right, the embryos will be shipped to your fertility clinic and you will arrive at your clinic for the transfer itself.

This is another opportunity for you and your spouse to be there for each other. On our transfer day, Julie and I asked if our friends back home could watch our sons for the day, and they graciously agreed. The doctor had instructed Julie to rest after the transfer, so we wanted to make sure our home environment would be just right upon our return. (Yes, husbands, this means you have yet another opportunity to step up and stand out on behalf of your wife. Chocolates, flowers—you know the drill.)

It's normal to be a bundle of nerves on the day of the big transfer. At least, I assume that's the case. I can only speak for myself, and I'm pretty sure Julie had to have been all butterflies, even though she handled it with ease. I tend to get stone-faced and somber when something of consequence is on my mind. Julie just smiles.

We arrived at the clinic and checked in. Our bubbly third-party coordinator placed us behind a curtain and had Julie don a hospital gown. She explained how the procedure would go. She threw in comment after comment about how excited she was and what great parents we would make (evidently, she didn't how our poor sons have fared) and how she hoped for the very best for us. She brought us an ultrasound photo of our embryo that would be transferred to Julie's uterus in just a few moments.

When the time arrived, we stepped inside the darkened operating room. Julie lay on the table and I sat on a chair next to her. Our doctor arrived in her scrubs and sneakers, and after a few pleasantries, she got down to the task at hand. A computer monitor faced Julie and me so we could watch the entire transfer unfold.

I will warn you that the intensity of the moment is stark. This is literally a life-and-death moment, and given that we had just learned only one embryo would be transferred, not two, we wanted everything to go perfectly. The doctor worked with stunning focus, preparing the environment around Julie's lower torso. Clearly, she'd done this procedure a time or two.

A door opened into an adjoining room, and a woman in a surgical mask stepped through. The doctor instructed her to bring the embryo, and a moment later she returned. They spoke to each other so everyone in the room could hear them confirm that the embryo in the straw belonged to Julie. Then the woman in the mask handed the doctor the vial attached to a long, thin tube.

Here's the really mind-blowing part: The doctor inserted the tube into Julie and, using her sense of touch and the monitor, directed it to Julie's uterus, where she successfully deposited our embryo and said as much out loud. I strained to see what she had pointed to on the screen but had a difficult time.

This living embryo, no larger than the period at the end of this sentence, had successfully survived close to a decade in sub-zero conditions, thawed, and was transferred to Julie's womb.

Whatever your perspective, a successful embryo transfer is a cause for celebration. From my view, this moment in our adoption journey reflected God's providential care for even the smallest members of his creation. As Jesus noted, "Are not five sparrows sold for two pennies? And not one of them is forgotten before God. Why, even the hairs of your head are all numbered. Fear not; you are of more value than many sparrows" (Luke 12:6–7).

After the transfer, our third-party coordinator wheeled Julie back to the recovery area. On TV, a 90s-and-loving-it Dick Van Dyke touted the benefits of Tai Cheng. His graceful exercise regimen brought a smile to my face. I reflected on Dick's excellent fitness and my own antimagnetic resistance to anything resembling a treadmill.

You will undoubtedly feel a little reflective after the transfer as well. You might not get the benefit of seeing Dick Van Dyke's smiling mug. You'll probably wonder what exactly led you and your spouse to this place, how it all happened so quickly, and why it seemed to take so long at the time.

Meanwhile, at the opposite end of life's spectrum, your embryo will begin the process of cozying up to her mommy and making herself comfortable. If everything goes according to plan, your nine-month journey will have only begun.

Discussion Questions

- If you are a soon-to-be adoptive mom, how will you prepare your mind and body for the medications that will be necessary ahead of your embryo transfer?

- If you are a soon-to-be dad, what are two to three things

you can do to remind your wife she is loved during this process?

- How will you make the events before, during, and after your embryo transfer memorable and restful? Who will you recruit, including your fertility clinic's staff, friends, and family, to ensure your transfer day goes smoothly and that your embryo has the best chance of implanting?

12

ARC OF AN UNCONVENTIONAL PREGNANCY

When we dream alone it is only a dream, but when many dream together it is the beginning of a new reality.

—Friedensreich Hundertwasser

In this chapter, you will learn

- How to endure the excruciating wait to determine whether your embryo transfer has successfully resulted in a pregnancy

- How pregnancy via embryo adoption is similar to, and different, from a conventional pregnancy

- Why your pregnancy represents the perfect time to get your house in order, literally and figuratively, so you will be ready to welcome your baby home

In a past life, I am quite sure I was a mole. The reason I know this is because I tend to get tunnel vision when I have a task in front of me. All of the background noises, all of the people, all of the distractions melt away, and the work at hand—which typically involves a laptop burning the midnight battery—consumes me. I might as well be a furry mammal digging a hole underground somewhere.

So you could have knocked me over with a feather one early morning as I worked away on my computer in the basement of our home. Days had passed since the embryo transfer, and in my typical state of mind, I had compartmentalized the event, realizing the success or failure of Julie's pregnancy would be entirely out of my control. I prayed hard, tried to give Julie the rest she needed, wrangled boys as often as possible, and kept my nose to the grindstone. Sometimes, a project keeps you from thinking about all of the worst-case scenarios that might unfold, how this pregnancy could be different, and awful, and end in tragedy.

Julie woke up and went into the bathroom, and I had an inkling this was no ordinary visit. A little while later, as I merrily clacked away on the keys, Julie walked down the hall and into our family room with a grin spread across her face.

"Well, are you ready for this?" she asked. "It's positive."

After stumbling over my initial shock, I jumped up and gave her a hug and kiss. After months of paperwork, consultations, meetings, doctor's appointments and, yes, painful buttocks shots, all of it had been worth it. Our baby had stepped onto the runway that would lead her (or him—we had no idea about gender, at that point) straight to the front door of the Birt household.

All of the patience you have cultivated up until this point will serve you well in the weeks and months ahead.

Before that first pregnancy test, it will feel as if you are holding your breath daily. A bunch of questions will race through your mind: Did the transfer go smoothly? Why do I feel as if nothing has changed? Or has something changed? Why didn't God give humans the incredible rapid-fire pregnancy experience of an American opossum, which brings forth young in just under two weeks?

If everything goes according to plan, you will then feel a rush of excitement a couple of weeks later when you take your first positive pregnancy test. Julie's initial test proved inconclusive, but she also didn't wait the prescribed time frame. Patience might be a virtue, but it's always a work in progress. Even after your first positive pregnancy test, your doctor's office will want to independently confirm the results with a follow-up test. The medical establishment needs to check Walgreens' math.

If you already have children, this will be old hat. If not, rest assured it's perfectly normal. Julie's follow-up proved to have the same outcome as the original: We were having a baby.

As time progressed, it became clear that certain aspects of this pregnancy would be the same as others, while other aspects would be totally different. Here's a quick rundown from my perspective as a dad who has encountered four pregnancies and four births. "Encountered" might sound a little distant, but I think it's more appropriate than "experienced" or "lived through" because those would imply I've personally endured physical pain and hardship. My wife will be the first one to tell you that's simply not the case. Here are my observations, and you can let me know if your own family's pregnancy experience looks similar or different:

- **Medicine requirements were more intensive early on with embryo adoption.** Julie temporarily continued taking estrogen pills after the embryo transfer. Additionally, she took progesterone shots for the first 10 to 12 weeks of pregnancy, and she had weekly ultrasounds with her fertility doctor until she had been authorized to return to her normal OB for appointments. If you are an expectant mom, your doctor's instructions will probably vary a bit. The bottom line here is that the post-embryo-transfer process varied quite a bit from the weeks after natural conception and early pregnancy.

- **Levels of morning sickness didn't fluctuate.** Julie never experienced severe morning sickness with her pregnancies, and embryo adoption proved no different. Expectant moms might find that the biggest causes of nausea are practices such as accidentally taking a multivitamin on an empty stomach or failing to eat something at regular intervals, including between meals. For those reasons, I'm not even sure why it's labeled as morning sickness. "All-day sickness" might be a better tagline. I doubt it will catch on because it sounds absolutely terrible. Moms, you're the best. Hang in there.

- **Heartburn persisted and worsened with time.** There's evidence that the more hair your baby will have, the worse your heartburn will be. Julie experienced this with all of our babies and purchased stock in an antacid factory as a result. Moms, you should probably become shareholders too, securing your own supply of pasty, acid-fighting spheres. (I'm kidding, of course. Seriously, though: Keep these magical, fake-fruit-tasting pills in stock. They're gross, but you can't afford an 11 p.m. run to the corner pharmacy every night.)

- **Bladder control wanes.** My wife is never going to let me write a book again after she reads this. But between you and me, I've been told that having a multipound weight sitting on top of your bladder 24/7 creates incontinence. You can manage it with low-cost tech from the pharmacy aisle of your local retailer, and no one will be any wiser, minus the cashiers, and they see this so many items every day they won't judge you. Promise.

- **The gender reveal is a source of perpetual excitement.** We couldn't believe it when our doctor told us we were having a girl. I've explained the reasons for this previously. In the next chapter, you'll see that our doctor was exactly right. Upon leaving the doctor's office on the day of our baby's gender check, we immediately drove over to Dollar General and purchased a pink bottle so we could surprise our in-town grandparents with the news. It was a happy day, and I'm confident your experience will be equally joyful, especially if this is your first baby. It makes your entire experience a little more real.

- **Your baby's movements will be unique.** Every baby behaves differently in the womb. Phoebe demonstrated her love of standing out by going breech on Julie and getting stuck in that position. This one really took us by surprise, and your baby will probably surprise you in ways entirely his or her own. In our case, the doctor didn't have a lot of hope Phoebe would turn upside down once more, and he was right. She represented our first breech baby, meaning her head pushed into Julie's lungs and restricted her ability to breathe for the final stretch of pregnancy. Phoebe also became our first baby delivered by C-section. As dearly as Julie loves her, she never wishes to experience a breech or a C-section again. I can't say that I blame her.

You can see that while some factors aren't too different

from a natural pregnancy, other aspects are quite different. Another difference really stems from your own special baby. Every person is different, even from a very early age, and those differences are known best by mommies everywhere.

Going into your pregnancy, fears will be understandable. This is acutely true if you have previously experienced miscarriages, or you have lost other embryos during the thawing process, or you are unsure what pregnancy will be like because you have never experienced it. But from our own personal experience and a reading of the scientific literature, you shouldn't expect your embryo baby to create a more difficult or volatile pregnancy than a baby from natural conception. I'm hopeful this will encourage you as moms and dads to ride the waves of pregnancy. Some days, you'll have tremendous joy as you reflect on the little person who will soon join your family. Other days, you moms will experience sickness, and you dads will need to do everything in your power to be supportive and ensure your wife is as comfortable as possible.

Each trimester brings its own atmosphere, according to firsthand questioning of my wife, who puts up with a lot of questions being married to a journalist. The second trimester is really the sweet spot. You are past the point of intensive morning sickness and adjustment to the pregnancy that occurs in the first trimester. Yet you aren't to the point where your baby has grown so large that you are experiencing difficulty breathing, or intensive heartburn, or extremely swollen feet caused by water retention. And as a dad, I can tell you definitively that you are nowhere near the point where your baby has a full grasp of the English language and can challenge your decision to withhold dessert for bad behavior. You can be really thankful you aren't at that point yet.

It's easy for me to tell you to soak up all of the joys of pregnancy like a sponge, but truthfully I've read things on social media and blogs that would curl your hair. Pregnancy isn't always a cheery, sun-baked beach where you romp across the sand and toss pebbles into the ocean. It can be akin to painful miles of walking on broken glass while carrying a bowling ball tucked into your undershirt. Celebrate the joy of life, but recognize that anyone who tells you to enjoy the moment probably hasn't been pregnant, simply enjoys being cruel, or honestly thinks physical pain is fun. In which case, they've probably met my runner brother, for whom pain is energizing. We all know that's just crazy.

Of course, if you are a pregnant mom, you aren't going to spend every waking moment exerting yourself physically, but you can use the time with your husband to get your house in order.

Part of this is literal, as in setting up your baby's room and neatening things up. Part of it is metaphorical, as in ensuring you are mentally ready for the changes that are coming.

You first-time dads should be aware of a phenomenon called nesting. It is where your wife seeks to replicate the life habits of a bird, which is essentially a robot with wings. Birds are so much on autopilot that they created a saying about them: birdbrained. I will draw no parallel between pregnant moms and birds other than to say that you should put your priorities on hold for at least eight months and ask your wife what you can do to help. If you have an especially good relationship, she might tell you. If your relationship is fair to middling, brace your chest for the mop handle that will be forced into it. Or your arm for the stepladder that will be hung from it. Or your mind for the honey-do list that will gently be foisted upon it.

The purpose of these activities is to create an optimal environment for your baby. More importantly, nesting creates an optimal environment for your wife, who will be stuck primarily in your home for several weeks after returning home from the hospital. As a dad, meanwhile, you will likely have the pleasure of spending hour after enjoyable hour at work, humming merrily through your day, and generally being enormously productive while your wife parents your infant, meaning feedings and changing diapers and losing sleep. If you've ever been under the impression life is fair, this will cure you. Support your spouse by doing these prebaby tasks and chores. You might never have washed the drapes as thoroughly as you are now, but believe me, you don't want this chore added to your list when your baby arrives and you've had a cumulative four hours of sleep over three days. Best to enjoy your rest now and do some of those tasks that bring your spouse joy.

More fun than nesting are activities such as building a gift registry for your baby, fawning over cute outfits and tiny socks at showers, setting up your baby's room, and learning whether your baby will be a boy or girl, if you choose to do so. The nine months of pregnancy are really a courtship between you as parents and your child. Every moment is precious, even though it might not feel like it at the time.

We started with a farm-themed room for our oldest son and have carried the theme through all four children. Julie's hand-drawn sketches of a cow, a chick, and a sheep hang in Phoebe's room above quilts pieced together over months by grandmas and family friends. Pink dolls, owls, and bunnies await the time when she will be old enough to cuddle with them in bed. Every onesie you fold and place into a drawer, and every animal you arrange along the foot of her bed, will remind you of the memories you will make in the months ahead.

Time can seem to drag on as your due date approaches. But in reality, you won't be able to stop its progression. Your baby will invariably arrive before every item on your worklist is checked off. Enjoy the experience of pregnancy because unless you plan to have a dozen or more children, these moments are fleeting. You'll spend a lot more time with your child out of the womb, telling them to go sit in a corner, stop drawing on the furniture, and think about your actions, mister.

One way you can speed yourself toward this beautiful, chaotic reality I have painted for you is by sleeping. Pregnancy proved for Julie to be exhausting. This meant taking plenty of naps and ignoring of alarms. I'm talking Sleeping Beauty-caliber snooze fests. As a husband—and you might appreciate this, men—I have been accused of sleeping through all kinds of important activities. Primarily, these involve sons screaming at 3 a.m. from the room above us, alerting us to urgent needs. These include blankets being lumpy on a bed, stuffed animals disappearing beneath cannibalistic pillows, or weeks-old wounds suddenly in need of antibiotic cream. I sleep right on through these, not because I'm heartless but because I am exhausted at day's end and have cultivated a subconscious ability to filter out tasks that Julie is better at doing. Or at least that is the story I tell myself.

A hard-nosed person might claim my wife had plenty of opportunities to catch up on sleep during her pregnancy. They might further claim all those naps gave her the endurance to personally handle late-night child-rearing sessions for the next 18 years of Phoebe's life. But of course, I would never say that. I'll just need Julie to elbow me whenever she needs help in the wee hours of the morning.

See what you're getting into? Let me tell you, losing sleep and changing dirty diapers might sound on the surface to be pretty dismal. But when you think about your embryo baby's journey, and the story you're writing together, it is pure magic.

So take a nap. Plan a date with your spouse. Put those finishing touches on the nursery.

You're all set to head to the hospital to welcome the baby you've been dreaming about.

Discussion Questions

- How will you manage the time between your first positive pregnancy test and your due date? List projects you'd like to accomplish in the interim, and sort them into "Must Complete" and "Would Like to Complete" categories, then pick the most important items in partnership with your spouse.

- What are two or three household chores or commitments you will agree to stop caring about during your pregnancy? Write down those things and tack them to your refrigerator or your bathroom mirror to remind yourself of the promise you've made. Read Jon Acuff's *Finish* for prebaby inspiration focused on setting reasonable goals.

- How will you and your spouse celebrate your time together as a couple before your baby's arrival? Set at least one date on the calendar for a date, a movie, or a weekend getaway.

PART V:
WELCOMING
YOUR EMBRYO BABY

13

SHOCKER IN THE OR

*All of my words, if not well put
nor well taken, are well meant.*

—WOODY GUTHRIE

In this chapter, you will learn

- How to create an embryo adoption elevator speech for those awkward moments

- Why it's critical to build relationships with embryo adoption champions

- What first-time parents can expect from their hospital stay

- How to manage expectations of doctors, nurses, and hospital staff to return home quickly

- How to socialize family and friends when your baby arrives

On the day Phoebe arrived, I strutted into the operating room where my wife lay on the table. I had covers over my shoes, scrubs on my body, and a hair net that made me look like a lanky cafeteria worker. It appeared a cast of thousands would be required to attend to Julie. She had so many drugs pumping through her veins that she slipped in and out of consciousness. You know those TV shows where a victim is wheeled down the hallway at 90 mph, doctors and nurses are shouting at one another because they clearly don't know who's in charge, and the victim's family member is trying to offer a soul-piercing word of moral support? That's exactly how it was.

I'm being dramatic. In reality, my wife is the one who should have been incensed. Phoebe became the first Birt baby to go breech, meaning she had to be delivered via C-section. This required the cast of *Grey's Anatomy*, an opioid cocktail that necessitated the hospital president's signature, and an uninvited tummy tuck. Or, rather, untuck.

Upon entering the room, the anesthesiologist offered me a stool, which I rolled next to Julie, keeping at a safe distance.

"You can get closer," the anesthesiologist offered.

As gently as possible, I rolled closer and positioned myself next to my wife's head for moral support. I held her IV-laced hand behind the blue veil of secrecy draped in front of her face.

Then the anesthesiologist called me a liar.

Embryo adoption might sound like a joke to some. Please assure them it is not.

Let me be clear: My wife to this day praises the kind anesthesiologist who delivered the spinal tap to deliver the drugs that minimized the pain of her OB cutting through layers of stomach tissue. But if we're being totally honest, the conversation didn't start well. After all, my wife was on drugs. She doesn't clearly remember this part.

It began innocently. The anesthesiologist had evidently taken some predelivery cheerleading classes because her role, it became clear, was to convince us that the next few minutes were going to be magical and perfect.

"Isn't this just exciting?" she said. "Mom, you're doing great. Do we know: is it a boy or a girl?"

We explained that our doctor, who stood nearby, had performed the ultrasound and declared the baby a girl. In fact, he'd told us he'd bet $100,000 on it in Vegas. ("If I only said $10,000, I wouldn't be so sure," he elaborated.) We also explained we weren't going to be convinced until we saw proof. After three boys, we were skeptics. Plus, small-town gossip suggested our doctor's predictions didn't always prove accurate. We're people of faith. But we're also Missourians. You have to show me.

She assured us she'd confirm the baby's gender as soon as she emerged from behind the painter's tarp. Then she abruptly shifted: "I can't wait to see which of you the baby looks like."

"Actually," I quipped, "she won't look like either one of us."

She laughed at that comment. Then she waved her hand as if brushing away a bothersome fly.

"No, seriously," I said. "She's adopted."

Then came the look of bewilderment, followed by a string of questions. "Oh wow," she said at one point, "it's like going to the pound to get a dog, only you get to keep it."

As you can imagine, after two years of praying and working, the moment we would meet our baby, those words hit me hard. But as the Woody Guthrie quotation at the start of this chapter notes, people often mean well even if they don't seem that way.

The conversation did improve. She spoke glowingly about our decision to adopt, about how cool embryo adoption is, about how she had never heard about it. Then came more words of support for Julie as the doctor and nurses worked to extract the baby.

First came a long little foot, then a little more—"I see girl parts!" the anesthesiologist gushed—and then Phoebe's whole body dangled briefly as the nurses prepared to swaddle her. She had evidently prepared for this moment because she started yelling and screaming as soon as she took that first breath.

I hated the fact that anyone would compare my daughter to a dog at the pound. So you can imagine how much I reveled in hearing that little yell. Phoebe had been a fighter from the moment she entered cryopreservation. Now, she would bring that liveliness to our family.

Anatomy of an Embryo Adoption Elevator Speech

If you and your spouse decide to adopt, you will have many opportunities to educate people. I kid you not. Some of the conversations are heartwarming. Some reveal new information that changes your understanding of people. "Oh, my grandfather was adopted," someone says. Or, with a far-off look in his or her eyes, another says, "I always wanted to adopt, but it never worked out." Still others, like my conversation in the operating room with the anesthesiologist, make your jaw drop.

You need prepare yourself. That doesn't mean you have to engage in a Twitter war or Lincoln-Douglas style debate or exploration of all the sides of a biological or moral question. But without having basic points that you can store in the world's number one cloud service—your own mind—you find yourself getting caught unprepared and unbalanced. When that happens, you easily become flustered and say statements you might regret later. (In chapter 14, I'll share some of our grandmothers' comments about adoption. Needless to say, they cross all kinds of boundaries. In moments like those, it helps to recall the fact you wouldn't be here without them.)

Before you craft your pitch, I would recommend doing the required reading your adoption agency provided. As you read, you'll notice a theme: talk openly about adoption, especially with your adopted child, but also with your other children, loved ones, friends, and so on. Adoption isn't something you discuss constantly to make your child seem different. The goal is to acknowledge openly and happily that your child's journey is as unique and important as that of anyone else. Do so naturally, not to make them feel isolated.

Next, think about how you can communicate that message. For example, imagine yourself in three years introducing your children to someone you've never met. If you have one adopted child and one biological child, you wouldn't ever say, "Here is my son, Timmy, and here is my adopted daughter, Emily." Instead, you would say, "Here are my children, Timmy and Emily." Not every situation requires a monologue on adoption.

Here is an example of an appropriate time to discuss adoption: Suppose you are at your baby's annual well checkup at the doctor's office. The nurse asks you to provide information about her family medical history. In that case, you might begin by saying, "Yes, I made sure to provide the doctor with a copy of her genetic (or placing) family's medical history. Specifically, there is a history of heart conditions." As her mom or dad, you want her to receive the best care possible. Concealing her identity simply by offering your biological family's history doesn't make sense.

Finally, you must rehearse the speech mentally. The specific words vary depending on 1) who is doing the asking, 2) the question itself, and 3) the context of the question (are you speaking in the privacy of your home, or are you at church with dozens of people nearby?). In the case of my experience with the anesthesiologist, I had been given ample opportunities before Phoebe's delivery to try variations on the same theme. I opted to speak about several key points:

- Most people don't know anything about embryo adoption, so I understand why you are confused.

- Parents who have gone through IVF and believe their remaining embryos are, in fact, human lives, store them securely. They may place the embryos with another family.

- The process is nearly identical to any other adoption. It is legal and governed by a detailed, binding contract.

- We have an open adoption, meaning we will foster a relationship with our daughter's placing family to ensure she knows her story and develops relationships as she grows older.

- Our names are on her birth certificate, and she is a Birt just like our three sons.

By answering several common questions before a person has the opportunity to ask them, you are establishing yourself as an expert in the subject. Remember that you don't have to know everything to be an expert. As Michael Hyatt, former chairman and CEO of Thomas Nelson Publishers, tells aspiring first-time authors, you can identify your own areas of expertise using the issues about which people constantly ask you questions as a guide. You didn't invent embryo adoption, but you've certainly read enough information, listened to webinars, and perhaps even started the adoption process.

As with any good line of questions, one leads to another. Most of the time, your elevator speech probably won't satisfy the other person's curiosity. You should listen for additional questions—and perhaps even the subtext of subsequent questions. For example, you will probably encounter people who enjoy drawing comparisons between features such as your hair color and your baby's hair color. The underlying premise of the question might be that family is determined exclusively by genetic identity. A polite response such as, "Yes, her hair is beautiful, isn't it?" allows you to acknowledge your baby's uniqueness without labeling her as different because she is adopted. Depending on the nature of the conversation, you might even take the opportunity to share your adoption journey and explain that you are thankful to your placing family for such a special gift.

You won't always be able to reply so thoughtfully, but you are capable of reading people's responses through their eyes, facial expressions, and word choices. Be proactive. This is a great opportunity to show grace, use humor and, in the worst-case scenarios, deflect inappropriate questions with poise.

By having an elevator speech prepared while keeping open the possibility of a constructive conversation, you gift your friends and family with new insights into embryo adoption. You also ensure you steer the conversation.

Find your own embryo adoption champions and embrace them.

For three of our four children, Phoebe included, we were blessed with Dr. Jones. You might not peg Dr. Jones as an OB if you saw him in public, but for those of us who know and love him, he is a family champion. He's also got a whole lot of

Midwestern charm. He raises hunting dogs. He has just the right amount of twang in his voice.

When Julie visited him for her required checkup as we began adoption paperwork, and he discovered what we were doing, he was instantly supportive. I can't count the number of times he told us how blessed our baby would be to be raised in our family, with us as parents. Julie and I make no excuses for the fact that we're far from the world's best parents. But there is something unequivocally inspiring about someone who doesn't owe you anything championing your cause, especially when that cause is so personal and stretches over so many months. We had three and could save the third embryo for a final transfer later. Plans change. But Dr. Jones did not. He didn't waver, and he provided us with gracious, sincere words of support before and after Phoebe arrived. He went further. Whereas some doctors would insist on transferring a single embryo—before we knew two would not survive the thaw— Dr. Jones noted he'd be comfortable transferring two at a time. He wasn't responsible for the transfer, but he was comfortable casting a decisive vote as the primary caregiver to Julie and our newborns.

I should mention he also ensured Julie and our baby stayed healthy throughout the delivery. More than that, he gave us the confidence we needed to keep going. His example is yet another instance where talking about your adoption journey, challenging though it might be at times, pays great dividends.

There are times when mandatory conversations, such as those with your doctor, lead to great partnerships and moral support. There are also times when you choose the people with whom you share the private details. Look for the people whose eyes light up or, if you're apart at long distances, whose tone via email or FaceTime shows you their genuine care. Surround yourself with kindness for the sake of your well-being. A few small words can be powerful as you build your family.

Early in our adoption, Julie and I relied on three sets of people to write letters recommending us as parents to our agency. I encourage you to find a similarly supportive group of people in your life because they will continually help you remember why you are taking this journey. Our group certainly did. First, we asked Dennis and Janie, close friends from our local church and adoptive grandparents to our children, to pen such a letter. They happily agreed. Next, we asked my brother, Adam, along with his wife, Jena. They offered their enthusiastic support of our efforts from the beginning. Finally, I asked my close college friend Greg, along with his wife, Kate. They represented another family we admire a great deal. They proved faithful in their friendship and ongoing support of our growing family.

Hospital Tips for First-Time Parents

If you've never had the privilege of spending the night in a hospital, and you are gearing up for the experience as a first-time adoptive parent, it's going to be really something. That's a polite way of saying it will be a combination of

- a vacation, in the sense you are removed from the daily grind

- an isolation chamber because you are completely removed from close friends and family

- a train station where doctors, nurses, and medical equipment are rolling in and out of your room around the clock on regimented schedules (occasionally, train is delayed or absent)

- a discount furniture store where all of the comfortable armchairs, beds, and sofas have already sold, leaving you with the loveseat with the cushion that slides swiftly toward your knees, turning your back into one side of an isosceles triangle as you try to doze

If all of this isn't appealing, it isn't supposed to be. Our local hospital does a tremendous job, but at the end of the day, it's a hospital. You enjoy the experience because you get to spend it with your embryo baby and your spouse. If you are the dad, your primary role is Champion of Mom. If you are the mom, your primary role is to slowly heal and politely delegate assignments to the Champion of Mom while your baby clings closely to your side (or other body parts, if you are breastfeeding).

Julie's delivery of Phoebe lasted perhaps six hours. We arrived at noon, and they had Julie complete reams of papers and prepare for the operating room. Surgery began at 1. By about 1:30 our baby arrived, after which I returned to the recovery room with Phoebe wrapped in a blanket. I admired her blue-gray eyes and her little tongue, which she flicked in and out like a lizard's, something I'd never seen our other children do. After the doctor stitched up Julie, she returned to the recovery room. Later, they transferred us to a new room. We began accepting visitors at about 6. You lose track of time in a hospital.

The message I want you mothers, in particular, to hear is that your doctor and nurses eventually check all of the boxes. As with anything in the adoption process, it takes time, and you will want some parts to speed up and end (e.g., the pain, the paperwork, the prep work) and others to slow down (e.g., the first time you hold your baby, your husband who is restlessly pacing the floor). Your experience will be different from our own, but I assure you there is a pace to it all, and your local hospital staff doesn't want you to be there any longer than necessary, just as you don't want to be there any longer than you have to be. Smile, say thank you, ask for whatever you need, use that little red button to call the nurse to up your dosage of painkillers if you need it, and sacrifice your good looks and modesty for a couple of days. There's a running joke in our house that the phrase "This too shall pass" should be banned because of a beloved family member known to use it frequently. But in this case, it really is true. Keep that realistic calendar in mind, and you'll be well positioned for a short stay.

Prioritize and answer post-adoption questions from your doctors, nurses, and accountants. Let's be honest: You won't ever actually settle into your hospital room. In the maternity ward, things are always in flux. Couples come and go, babies are born and begin growing, and someone in accounting keeps ringing the cash register. This is business, after all. If you are blessed enough to be situated in a rural hospital as we were, the pace will likely be much slower, but you'll still have regular check-ins from nurses making sure your wife's vitals are stable, your baby's hearing gets checked, and so on.

A hospital encounter after Phoebe's arrival leads me to offer you some unsolicited advice on dealing with people. (Remember, I'm a journalist, so use your discretion. My friends and I in the news media don't exactly have the most stellar reputation, even though I tend to be biased in their favor.) In all our childbearing years, Julie and I had never had the privilege of visiting with the hospital's accountant. A knock on the door on the day after Phoebe's arrival changed that.

The bubbly woman carried a clipboard and made small talk about our adorable daughter and her delighted big brothers.

Then, smile firmly fixed on her face, she arrived at the point of her visit: "How will you be paying for this?"

We explained we intended to pay cash for whatever our insurance didn't cover. She admonished us to contact our insurer immediately—preferably an hour ago—to ensure Phoebe had proper coverage. She reminded us of her joy over our new arrival before again urging us to contact our insurer. I assured her I would take care of it. After all, our baby had only just arrived. After exchanging a few more pleasantries, she returned to her office.

Thankfully, I had done my homework on this, and so can you. You should visit with your employer a couple months ahead of your hospital stay and determine exactly what documentation your insurer needs. Make sure you get, in writing, confirmation your insurer covers adopted children. (Embryo adoptions are unique because babies are delivered to the adoptive mother directly, so the parents' name goes directly on the birth certificate. But it never hurts to be safe.) Also determine if you need to simply provide details online, as I did, or file official life-event paperwork. That way, you can ensure any needed websites or documents are accessible.

Within five minutes of our accountant's visit, I completed the appropriate form. I called her and confirmed I had submitted Phoebe's details. Her voice held a hint of surprise—and perhaps gratitude that I had unexpectedly followed her instructions. Remember what I've said about building relationships: you might never see this person again, but you just never know. The little things can make a big difference and ensure your hospital stay goes smoothly.

One final note is you should always ask about discounts for paying early, and double-check if you are told there are none. We initially paid the full amount after getting our bill via email about a month later. Then the paper bill arrived and stated that we'd receive a $50 discount for paying early. Julie nudged me to call the hospital, and the billing department gladly refunded us. You're welcome. Use the money for diapers.

Clearly, conversations about finances and insurance are ones you should be having, even if they seem to sap some of the magic from your baby's arrival. You wouldn't be holding your beautiful baby were it not for the hospital's help. Express your gratitude by paying what you owe.

You should know there is nothing wrong with encounters like this. It is perfectly acceptable to set boundaries and politely conclude a conversation before it gets started. In fact, if you haven't read *Boundaries* by Drs. Henry Cloud and John Townsend, I highly recommend it. Allowing yourself to say no gives you opportunities to say yes when it really counts.

Socialize your family and friends to your baby's arrival. For those of you who already have children, what I'm about to say is obvious. If you haven't yet welcomed children into your home, hopefully it at least reinforces a few basic tools that help you handle well-meaning family and friends.

First, you don't need to have anyone but your spouse in the delivery room with you. In fact, if it's a C-section like Julie had, your doctor probably won't allow it, anyway. Your family and friends will have plenty of opportunities to visit with you and your new baby. Turn off your devices. This is a big event, and you don't want to miss it because your eyes are bathed in the blue light of your smartphone.

Second, you are under no moral or legal obligation to open your doors to guests as soon as the nurses wheel your wife from the delivery room. Spend time together with your new baby. Relish the moment. Unless you are intent on having a dozen or more children, these experiences are rare. There's something especially touching about an embryo baby. You'll reflect on where they've been for the past several years and on the many opportunities ahead of your baby and your family. It's likely that for quite some time, your baby remained frozen near absolute zero at one-tenth of a millimeter in size. Today, you are holding your warm, snuggly baby in your arms.

Third, communicate with your spouse before the guests arrive. As a husband, I sometimes read my wife's body language well, and other times I do so imperfectly. If your wife feels sick while guests parade through your room, your day is probably going to go poorly—if not for them now, then for you later. You don't need to overshare with your guests. Simply explain that your spouse is tired, the baby needs rest, and as much as you love them, you'll see them soon.

Last, be good to yourself. Under the best circumstances, you will probably spend 48 hours or less in the hospital. When you're experiencing each hour, though, time drags. Close your eyes when you can—guys, don't use this as an excuse to check out when your wife needs you most—and don't feel bad if the nurse offers to take your baby to the nursery so you can sleep. Julie and I declined with our older sons, but by the time number three and Phoebe rolled around, we didn't hesitate. We loved them all dearly, but we knew our limitations better. To provide them with the best care, we needed to be our best selves, and sleep is an essential part of that.

Speaking of which, good night.

Discussion Questions

- Envision your own baby's birth. What do you imagine the experience will be like? Picturing that special day will give you hope that this process has a wonderful outcome.

- Who in your life may be outstanding champions for your adoption journey? Think about people you've met so far, perhaps even known for years, who would support you from the beginning. Make them an important part of the upcoming weeks and months. Look to them for encouragement more than anything. They are here for you.

- What do you need to do to prepare for the delivery and birth of your baby? You might need to leave instructions for taking care of your home or a pet. You'll need to make arrangements at work and perhaps speak with your insurance company. Make a to-do list ahead of your hospital stay and pick something each day to complete. By the time of your delivery, you might not have everything completed, but you'll have the most important tasks finished. If you are a mom, remember: delegating to your husband is perfectly acceptable and encouraged.

- How will you prioritize questions and instructions from your doctors and nurses? Remember the instructions in this chapter. If it has to do with money, you should probably take care of it. Your insurer's instructions for getting your baby signed up for health care should be relatively straightforward. If, on the other hand, the hospital chaplain asks, "Is there anything I can do?," and you genuinely have no needs, simply say no. Chances are good you have a community all your own for spiritual and moral support.

- What boundaries should you set with your family and friends to ensure everyone's introduction to your baby goes as smoothly as possible? Remember, moms: you are recovering from an intensive medical procedure, regardless of whether your baby is delivered vaginally or via

C-section. Don't shy away from turning away guests or simply having your husband warn people via text message that it isn't a good time to visit. You will have plenty of time together after you return home, and you'll all probably enjoy the experience more then, anyway.

14

FACT AND FICTION

Blessed is the man who, having nothing to say, abstains from giving us wordy evidence of the fact.

–George Eliot

In this chapter, you will learn

- Why you should not need to worry about an imminent kidnapping of your adopted baby, contrary to popular belief

- What some popular misconceptions about your baby's genetic heritage are and how to respond, or avoid responding, to those beliefs

- How to cultivate familiarity and appreciation for your placing family among loved ones who are coming to terms with your decision to adopt

During elementary school, a group of friends and I developed a weird obsession with a storm drain near the playground. I can't imagine what drew us to this concrete cylinder in the ground covered with a big metal grate. But it entranced us, and suddenly a mythology had sprung from the depths of the ground that became difficult to contain.

"There's a baby trapped down there," my friend Heather pleaded. "She's bloody and she's crying."

All of us stood around the perimeter, staring into the drain. Sure enough, we could hear faint cries and imagine that poor suffering baby lying cold and abandoned in the sewer. We became so concerned we called over one of the teachers, who looked into the drain, didn't see anything, and encouraged us to go be normal. Eventually, we did.

The moral of this story is simple: We've all imagined worst-case scenarios, and in some cases even convinced ourselves of realities that are downright lies. Spread the lie long enough and it becomes a believable narrative. With each retelling, an innocent story becomes a laughable yarn and eventually morphs into something that becomes a little bit like a boa constrictor, eating all of the truth in its path and sowing confusion.

I hate to break it to you after you've just brought your beautiful baby home, but you will probably encounter a little of this artful storytelling—and questioning—as an adoptive parent. Julie and I sure have. In the last chapter, we talked about some of those ideas and misconceptions that cropped up, literally beginning in the delivery room.

Once you return to your home environment, you are not immune. The doors of your family are open for business. You can bet loved ones from all walks of life and with all kinds of ideas about the nature of reality are going to learn of your adoption story, bring it up, and be bold with you. This might sound daunting, but I want to encourage you that it creates dozens of teachable moments.

Remember what the end result of all of this will be: more families will learn about embryo adoption because of you, and more babies will have the possibility of new life as a result.

In the short-term, though, it's time to shore up your teaching and myth-busting skills.

Some are pretty innocent. Others are downright laughable. But the majority of those questions come from an honest place. The people who love you and your family most want what's best for you. Keep in mind the embryo adoption process is probably as new for them as it is for you. You're both trying to navigate a giant maze with a keychain flashlight.

In no particular order, here are some of the most popular misconceptions Julie and I have encountered since Phoebe has been a visible part of our family. For each, I've included some thoughts on ways you can respond to people whose beliefs aren't aligned with reality.

Myth 1: Because you adopted your baby as an embryo, your placing family might not have developed a strong attachment. Now that your baby is born, her genetic family will see how cute she is and take her back. My initial response to this one is a big chortle, mainly because I can envision an entire family trying to scale a house in the dark of night and stealthily slip inside to kidnap a baby. I envision them all wearing trench coats, weaving one by one down an ivy-covered lattice to their escape vehicle. It sounds like something out of a celebrity crime story *The New York Times* might have splashed above the fold circa the 1940s.

The sad part about this misconception is it fails to account for the emotional turmoil families with extra embryos face before they even decide to place them. For those who believe each embryo represents a human life, the decision to consider adoption necessarily involves separation.

You can explain to your loved ones that in many cases, couples freeze embryos and pay monthly fees to ensure they are stored until they are comfortable placing them. In some cases, perhaps couples simply pay the fee and forget about them. I suspect, though, that many parents choose to keep their embryos preserved because they recognize their inherent value. They are working toward the point when they can emotionally and spiritually place them in full confidence, trusting God to shepherd the adoption process. Sometimes, that process takes years or even decades.

Another factor that provides security both to placing and adopting families, and eases fears of a court battle, is the process of giving legal consent. Embryos legally are considered property in most of the United States. In states such as Louisiana, embryos are recognized as people, a designation I am hopeful will become the rule and not the exception in the years ahead. Regardless, the legal process of adoption offers safeguards both to placing and adoptive families. The placing couple may decide to push the Pause button on the adoption for whatever reason at multiple points in the process. If the couple decides to continue, they sign a legally binding contract. The adoptive parents sign a similarly legally binding contract securing their parenting rights. Our adoption agency even gave us the option of consulting our personal attorney to review the contract in case we had questions or wanted a second opinion.

In the past, some people exclusively referred to the process of moving embryos from one family to another as a donation. This is still the case at many fertility clinics, and it is an option you can consider as an alternative avenue for embryo adoption. But though adoption comes with modest costs, including home-study visits and embryo shipping, I firmly believe it is the best option for your child.

Agencies rightly point out the embryo-adoption process provides legitimacy to any children resulting from pregnancy. The purpose of your contract, and really the entire adoption process, is to provide any children that are born through embryo adoption the legitimacy of any other adopted child.

It places less emphasis on the transaction between placing and adopting family and more emphasis on adoption being a permanently transformational event for the welfare of the adopted child. Not only that, but also it is an adoption for four key reasons, explains Daniel Nehrbass, Ph.D., president of Nightlight® Christian Adoptions:

1. You are parenting a child who is not related to you.

2. There is an open relationship.

3. There is a home study.

4. Matching occurs and is done by a social worker.

Your friends might also be surprised to learn couples that place their embryos often have other older children and might be past the point of raising more children. It could be because their doctor has told them they can't physically bring more babies to term.

The good news for your fearful friends is embryo adoption can a lifelong process of cultivating a relationship with your placing family. It can also be closed or anonymous, depending on your preference. It isn't a heat-of-the-moment decision that placing parents quickly jump into or out of—and once you've committed, you're in it for life. So if someone asks you whether you're afraid they'll take back your baby, I want to encourage you that fear should have no place in your response.

If you are in an open adoption, explain that you are getting to know your placing family, that you cherish them and your budding relationship, and that you will do everything with the best interest of your baby at heart.

Myth 2: Embryo adoption involves medical processes that fuse an adopted egg with a husband's sperm. This is one of those "heard it through the grapevine" notions that we heard from one of our beloved older relatives. I normally wouldn't call out someone's age, but in this case you should keep in mind this really is a generational issue. IVF hasn't been around all that long, and our grandparents never had access to technology that could fuse sperm and egg in a laboratory. The misconception here stems from a real practice, known as egg donation, where a woman donates her eggs to a couple and then the couple uses the husband's sperm to create an embryo. The embryo is then transferred to his wife's womb.

The distinction between egg donation and embryo adoption is that with embryo adoption, you are adopting an embryo that already has the genetic contribution of both the placing mom and dad. From a Christian viewpoint, many argue that this is akin to adopting a child who has already been carried to term. By contrast, many Christians believe, couples find themselves in a moral dilemma when they choose to use only a donated egg, or only donated sperm, to bring a baby into the world. The reasoning goes that Jesus spoke about the importance of marriage being between one man and one woman for life, whereas a donated egg or sperm brings a third party to the relationship, albeit at the cellular level. The couple's child will bear one parent's genetic traits but not the other's. I don't profess to be an expert in theology, but you can study your Bible, perform additional research online, and ask people whose expertise in these matters you respect. Embryo adoption avoids these questions because you are adopting a baby at its earliest stages of life. It is a child who only needs a maternal womb to develop and to be born.

You should know, though, that many embryo adoption agencies do ask whether you are comfortable adopting embryos created through donor eggs or donor sperm. Julie and I said we would be comfortable because we believe all embryos deserve a chance at life, regardless of how their parents decided to create them. As a married couple, our criterion was to seek existing embryos, rather than trying to create an embryo from the start. Adoption options vary, and every couple needs to decide what is right for them. Boundaries vary for all of us. My purpose in sharing this is to ensure you have a basic overview to begin making your own decisions.

Myth 3: Embryo adoption is the same as surrogacy. Unlike surrogacy, in which a woman carries a baby to term on behalf of another family, embryo adoption involves the adoptive mother carrying the baby to term and becoming his or her parent for life.

Myth 4: Your baby looks just like you because you are genetically related. Sweet little Phoebe inherited a gorgeous head of strawberry-blonde hair. Out in the sunlight, it appears to glow. There's no mistaking that red tint, and it's often the first thing people comment on.

"Look at that red hair," they'll say. "She's beautiful. Which side of your family does that come from?"

The irony is not lost on Julie's family, which has a history of people with ginger hair over generations past. As with our anesthesiologist whom you met in an earlier chapter, people who learn Phoebe is adopted express a little shock. If she is out shopping with Julie, folks often comment on how alike they look. These comments are especially amusing, and it's rarely necessary to have a lengthy adoption conversation. It's an opportunity to smile, say thank you, and laugh a little under your breath. Well-meaning people are trying to bond with your baby and pay you a compliment, and it's no time to start an argument. You can always pick up the conversation later.

Myth 5: You can't breastfeed a baby who isn't genetically related to you. Julie and I are unsure where this idea came from. But rest assured, if you adopt an embryo baby, and you are blessed with the ability to do so, breastfeeding would happen naturally for both parties involved. Phoebe has been an eager breastfeeder, and while we occasionally give her a bottle for convenience, particularly if Julie is away from home, she'll take a breastfeeding session with her mommy any day.

Myth 6: Your adopted baby's family will always be a mystery to your daughter as she grows up. I addressed this one in myth 1, but it bears repeating: Having an open adoption means you can build as close a relationship as you like. Every family still needs boundaries and borders, but remember you are building a life for your baby. You have every right to keep in touch with your placing family via text message, email, social media, phone, in-person visits—whatever your families mutually agree is acceptable and comfortable. It's even possible to change the ways you stay in touch as time goes on.

Myth 7: You adopted your baby because you knew she would be a girl. You already know I'm a sucker for a little princess, but we had no idea Phoebe would be a girl. For months after the gender-reveal ultrasound, I braced myself for a little boy, the latest addition to our pickup basketball team. Our agency even had us sign a contract stating we would not genetically test our embryos to determine their gender. It turns out you must thaw your embryo, take a cell sample, and then refreeze the embryo to do this testing. That can put your baby's life at risk. Further, giving parents the ability to choose which embryos to keep and which to destroy based on gender, or any medical abnormalities, runs counter to the Christian worldview. For those reasons, your agency might also prohibit the practice. Our adopted baby's gender proved just as surprising as the gender of our three biological sons.

Once you've heard these myths or others more than once, you'll fall into a routine of deciding whether to offer a rebuttal or simply let them roll off your back.

For the most part, I'd recommend the latter. If you know someone really well, it doesn't hurt to give them some helpful pointers or clarifying facts. But before you begin recruiting them for embryo adoption advocacy campaigns, I would advise first helping them love your placing family as much as you do.

Few activities will be more important to your child's future than normalizing your placing family's special place of honor in your life. Share updates from your placing family with your closest family members as appropriate, share photos of their family so your loved ones get to know them, and explain why you are building a lifelong relationship—to help your child understand her heritage and have access to all of the people who love her and want her to understand her story fully.

Don't overshare, and don't hesitate to be picky about which topics you discuss with your loved ones. One way I keep our loved ones in the loop with our placing family is to occasionally show them a photo on my phone of Phoebe's genetic siblings. I always enjoy imagining what our children will look like when they grow up, and Phoebe's genetic siblings give me a peek into the future, just as our oldest son, Micah, gives me a peek at what our youngest son, Ezra, might look like.

Your purpose is to make your relationship with your placing family routine so your extended family views them as simply another part of themselves. Not everyone knows how to react to the addition of an entirely new family unit to their own, but your small gestures of compassion and kindness will set a powerful example for your family and your child.

We've sorted out some common misconceptions from the truth. Let's now explore some ways you can bring your newly blended family closer together. I guarantee it will involve a whole lot of hugs and snuggles.

Discussion Questions

- What are some of the most common misunderstandings you've heard about your own adopted child? Realize many people don't intend any harm. They simply want to connect with you and your baby.

- How can you use the information you've learned in this chapter to either start a conversation with someone who raises an uninformed question, or simply move along? What criteria will you use to decide when and how to respond?

- Based on how your extended family stays in touch with one another, how will you normalize your relationship with your baby's placing family? Think about one update you can share in the next week that will help your loved ones appreciate the special role your placing family plays in your life.

15

BLENDED DESTINY

What is a child, monsieur, but the image of two beings, the fruit of two sentiments spontaneously blended?

—Honoré de Balzac

In this chapter, you will learn

- How to help your biological children* understand what it means to be adopted and to have an adopted sibling

- Why a blended family can be a tremendous opportunity for your children to understand the values of respect and diversity

- Why it's important to allow your blended family to simply become a family with a feeling of total normalcy and comfort

---

* If you don't have biological children, you're welcome to skip this chapter and move to the final section of the book. That said, if you intend to have more than one child in the future—adopted, biological, or even foster—you might find the in-formation in this chapter helpful.

Cousins made my childhood summers memorable. Every other year, Mom and Dad loaded up the minivan at our home in Colorado and headed east for the land of their upbringing. Generally, the trip began in rural Middle Tennessee, where my mom grew up. My grandparents, known to us as Mamaw and Grandpa, lived on over 30 acres of land. We rode through the fields with Grandpa on his blue Ford tractor, watched Mamaw deep fry okra and prepare meatballs by hand, and chased cousins across the wraparound porch of their Revolutionary War-era home.

On that porch, I had my first up-close experience with what it means to be a blended family. My uncle Stephen, aunt Angie, and cousin Daniel had adopted a little girl, Kara, from South Korea. I vividly remember sitting on the red-and-white metal patio glider on my grandparents' backyard porch, rocking and gently stroking Kara's black hair as she slept. This baby looked nothing like the white family she had been adopted into, and yet it seemed as if providence had made a point of placing her in our lives at exactly the right time.

You will feel the same way about your embryo baby. And if you do a little conditioning of your biological children, they will welcome her with open arms.

I honestly didn't know if this would be the case. Mostly, this is because a doctor told me in the early stages of the process that I had made a bad bargain.

I'm exaggerating, but only just. It all started when our adoption agency told Julie and me that we needed to get a checkup. The medical community needed to provide evidence of our ability to successfully parent an adopted child. The fact our three biological sons had survived infancy and seemed to be thriving had no bearing. You can't look at your son and determine whether your heart will give out in the next calendar year.

Being me, I scheduled a well visit for myself as soon as I could find my way to a smartphone. I didn't want to wait around. If this paperwork would be a barrier between me and my little bundle of joy, I would dispose of it as quickly as possible.

The visit went remarkably smoothly. I sat in the waiting room underneath a vaulted ceiling and within a few paces of a fish tank. Fish at a doctor's office seem to perform on cue, swimming merrily along. It's as if they've resolved to keep a stiff upper lip despite being surrounded by sick people, insurers, and piles of bills.

The nurse took me back and took my vitals. The doctor soon followed and struck up a conversation. I explained how I had scheduled an appointment as part of our efforts to adopt.

"How many kids do you have?" she said.

"Three," I explained.

"Good luck with that," she said. "My parents had foster children all my life. They adopted when I was seven, and I couldn't wait to get out of there."

The doctor went on to explain how awfully the siblings in her blended family had behaved, and how her parents' attention had been diverted to children causing trouble. She wished me the best but made it pretty clear Julie and I were walking into a field littered with land mines.

For the first time, I realized not all blended families work functionally, and not everyone thinks a blended family is even the best idea.

I used to categorize blended families mainly as those whose parents had been divorced and remarried, bringing new siblings into the mix as a result. Today I know that blended has many more nuances. There are plenty of families with children who have been adopted or fostered. Others are grandparents who are watching their grandchildren while their own children get back on their feet. And the list goes on.

Although blended families might come with their own set of challenges, the notion that family is complicated and often difficult is true of every family I've ever known. If someone tries to discourage you before or after your embryo adoption on the basis that you won't be able to make it work, ignore their urgings. I assure you, it is possible to have a happy life even though your child isn't biologically your own.

In fact, one of the advantages of embryo adoption we've already discussed in this book is that you know your baby from the womb. You build a deep bond with your baby. Your adoptive relationship is inherently unique because of the point in time at which you bonded. There's no question some children who have spent years in and out of foster care, or being passed from family to family, or have experienced horrific abuse and injustice, have special needs families must accommodate. I can't imagine how difficult that must be. Even in cases like that, though, I guarantee you there are families who have made it work and would tell you it was worth it, despite the heartache they sometimes faced.

We helped our children become comfortable with adoption by discussing it frequently over dinner.

It didn't involve a long, protracted, and scientific conversation about Phoebe's backstory. We simply initiated conversations about bringing another baby into our family and about the special placing family that made it possible because they believed her life had meaning and purpose.

Those stories entranced the boys, and today their sister is a

Birt through and through. Now that Phoebe can hold her head up, smile, and coo at the boys, they are absolutely in love. When we place her in her Bumbo seat so that we can finish preparing dinner in the kitchen or pack the diaper bag for Sunday worship, the boys are drawn to her like flies to honey. Titus in particular knows no personal boundaries. He goes nose to nose, chattering at Phoebe and jerking his elbows this way and that, which gets Phoebe squealing and giggling within seconds. The rest of us roll our eyes and urge Titus to calm down before he does too much and scares the baby, but this special language of theirs is a powerful example of a bond that crosses bloodlines.

Perhaps the most compassionate of all is Micah who—despite his frequent refrain that "cuties don't cry"—feels an enormous draw toward his little sister. Before her birth, he spoke to her in Julie's womb. Today, he begins running toward her and shouting, "Phoebe!" at first sight, while Julie plays second fiddle and perhaps gets a hug after his sibling greeting. "You're so cute!" Micah proclaims.

Meanwhile, Ezra shares a special trait with his sister that his brothers do not: a dimple square in the middle of his left cheek. He tends to sport it when he beams as his sister comes into view. "Phoebe, Phoebe, Phoebe!" he yells.

In the mornings, the boys mob me as I make my way to Sissy's room to exchange her pajamas for a onesie. Invariably, a fight ensues over who will pick out her bow for the day, and Titus usually wins, rushing to her closet and beginning a mad dig through her gray farm-themed treasure box in the closet. One day recently, they all worked in tandem to force socks onto her feet. Titus found a pair of tiny sneakers and managed to mold the edges to fit around her ankles. It won't surprise you to learn they were on the wrong feet. His proud grin extended from ear to ear.

All of these experiences will help your children appreciate the value of diversity as they get older.

As a member of our local school board, I've had the pleasure of interacting with many different families, and I can tell you that no two are alike. Our children are enrolled in public school, and I have no doubt they will encounter people from many different backgrounds from the youngest ages on through college and into the workforce.

Rather than assuming everyone acts like you, looks like you, and believes like you, they will know firsthand that you can care about people who aren't exactly the same. Their sweet redheaded sister is testament to the fact that families stick together, even if it means she must bond with three sweet but stinky brown-haired brothers.

My career as a journalist has taken me to some amazing places, and my travels are pretty mundane compared to those of the truly adventurous. I've toured dairies in rural China, stood mesmerized by the Vancouver skyline, seen the restaurant that inspired Goethe's *Faust* in Germany, and strolled past New York's ornate Rockefeller Center tree at Christmastime.

I hope your travels and experiences have taken you to places even more amazing than that. But even if you've never spent time far outside your hometown, chances are probably good that your child will venture farther than you've ever imagined—if not in person, then virtually. Technology will enable future generations greater exposure to the wonders of the world in ways none of us have ever thought about. That means it is your responsibility as a parent to expose them to the diverse cultural heritage of our world so they can be prepared to learn from others and show love. If you are a Christian like I am, you also believe the Bible has a particularly important message for our culture today. For our children to bring that message to the world, we must first be willing to engage the people of the world in the way they deserve to be treated.

One of the beautiful things about embryo adoption is that you get to chart this type of course for your children from the very beginning.

Rather than making your children feel different because of their unique birth stories, you can celebrate them for who they are. Every parent envisions what his or her child's future might look like. But you can enjoy every moment as it arrives, even as you look further ahead. You can applaud your children's character: their love for others, their work ethic, their curiosity, their ability to ask good questions, and their selflessness. There are virtually unlimited ways to speak truth into the lives of your children without resorting to the kinds of compliments that too often hurt our children more than help.

Yes, your children are handsome or beautiful. Yes, they are good at X or Y activity. But you and I are not responsible for cultivating beauty kings and queens, or all-star activity doers. You and I are tasked with building families whose children have the strength of character and passion for life to make a difference in the world, help others, and live with humility and purpose. Because that is the type of person you have become if you have made the decision to step into embryo adoption. You understand at your core that humanity is worth the fight. When the going gets tough, as the saying goes, the tough get going.

We are about to embark on the final leg of our journey together, and I want you to know it will be an encouraging one indeed. The tears you have cried, the work you have committed, the bonds you have built will all produce the fruits of opportunity in your adopted child's life. Let's explore together how we can build a future with our adopted children that will make them especially proud. Let's work hard to provide them with a world of opportunities for incredible success.

Discussion Questions

- What are two or three conversation starters about adoption you might use over dinner or another family time with your biological children? What are the most important things you want them to know about the important place they and their adopted siblings hold in your lives as parents?

- Have you ever thought about your family as a blended one? How does that change the way you think about the important perspective your family will give your children as they grow up?

- How will you use your own newfound perspective on adoption and family to fuel your support of other parents, adoptive families, and causes you believe in?

PART VI:
NAVIGATING YOUR NEWBORN'S EARLY DAYS

16

NEITHER YOUR EYES
NOR YOUR SMILE

*No one is ever really a stranger. We cling to the belief that
we share nothing with cer-tain people. It's rubbish. We have
almost everything in common with everyone.*

—Mark Haddon

In this chapter, you will learn

- How to enjoy parenting a newborn, whether for the first
  time or not

- Ten parenting rules that will help you serve your child's
  needs, and your own, in the moment rather than regretting all of the things you don't have the bandwidth to
  accomplish

- How networking with other parents in person and via
  social media helps you take yourself less seriously and
  provides you with an important check on the reality of
  raising children

Every day as a parent, you put on your fighting gear. Whether you think of yourself as a boxer, a gladiator, or simply as a mom in kneepads, you've got the toughest job in the marketplace. I'm a fighter, too, though I generally think of myself as a martial artist with limited weaponry save for my deadly fists and razor-sharp intellect. Other than that, I've got nothing.

I think the fuel firing my parenting journey ignited beginning in social studies class at Westview Middle School. I know this sounds odd, so please bear with me. I have never been accused of having pristine logic.

I had the same set of teachers in the core subjects for all three years, and I generally adored my teachers. Looking back, I particularly admire their patience, encouragement, and gentle spirit in spite of the often-tumultuous teenage years. My social studies teacher, Mr. Tafel, took his work seriously. That meant ensuring his students learned about the amazing story of our past. He knew his facts, he had a commanding voice, and he had a great laugh. His sense of humor meant he didn't take himself too seriously, and it enabled him to work with even the most difficult kids.

But one day in his classroom, I got really peeved. I didn't jump up on my desk and call him out for what he'd said. It shook me to my core, though, and it's stuck to my mind like glue for the better part of 20 years. You are going to think this is silly, but I will tell you what he said:

"You are the first generation in the history of this country who will not be as successful as your parents." Specifically, he was referring to financial success. Evidently, he'd read something in the newspaper or studied some research suggesting that people like me—affectionately called Old Millennials, as if that somehow distances us from the allegedly grating, whiny, ungrateful Young Millennials—would fall off the economic wagon.

His words immediately took me to a dark place. Did this mean we'd all be taking hourly jobs mopping gas station floors? Would we all cling to the hope that lottery tickets would be our only way to financial freedom? Would our parents hang their heads in shame, knowing the deck had been stacked against us from the moment we scream-greeted the world from the delivery room?

I didn't know the first thing about making money or fighting the Federal Reserve, but I sure didn't plan to let Mr. Tafel dictate what I would or wouldn't do with my life. I still wonder sometimes whether my teacher planted those comments like a burr under the saddle of a horse. If he had that plan in mind all along, let me tell you that it worked beautifully.

There have been a few other moments in my life that stick out vividly as turning points when I knew I needed to ratchet up my game. That one time in middle school, though, proved the catalyst for all of it. I'll never forget Mr. Tafel because he gave me the opportunity to prove him wrong.

Adoption will give you the opportunity to set the record straight on all sorts of levels, starting with your own precious embryo baby.

Your infant has no preconceptions about what good parenting looks like. He doesn't even know you aren't his genetic parents. I'm not suggesting you try to hide this fact at any point in your adoptive parenting journey, but what I am saying is your baby will adore and cherish you because you are all he has ever known.

Especially if this is your first baby, you will learn a great deal by trial and error as you go through the first few weeks and months. Here are some of the most important things I've been learning (or relearning) as Phoebe's dad, and I hope they can benefit you too:

Rule 1: Just because your baby doesn't have your eyes or your smile doesn't mean she isn't yours. Recall that hesitation I felt way back in chapter 13 in the delivery room? I almost didn't know if it was all right to touch my baby because, after all, her life had begun away from Julie and me. Don't buy into that idea. If you are an in open adoption, you have journeyed with your placing family to the point at which you can hold your baby in your arms. Your placing family longs for that baby to have a loving home, and I've got a message for you: *You* are that loving home. Savor each moment with your baby. You will always be her parents, legally and literally. Parenting is a job description, not a biological marker.

Rule 2: You're working with a living human being, and humans can be broken. There will be times exhaustion overtakes you, and you will need to ask your spouse to step up and step in because you've simply done as much as you can. I've been there many times, and it's nothing that should cause you shame. The first few weeks with a newborn can be like living in an insomniac's nightmare. When you want to sleep, your baby is awake. When your baby is asleep, you can't figure out an artful way to put him down in his crib so you can catch a few winks.

With exhaustion comes an inability to make thoughtful decisions that could directly affect your child's health and well-being. The admonition you should never shake a baby is exactly right, and yet in times of frustration, it's easy to see how this life-or-death advice is ignored. Never forget the fact that you have a network of people who want the best for your baby and are happy to help. If you don't have a network or live in a remote area where people are few and far between, lean on your spouse for support. Use the internet or resources from your local library for ideas about ways to safely care for your baby while managing the stresses you face day to day.

Rule 3: Babies offer second chances. My attitude sometimes needs serious repairs. Lack of sleep, frustration over something at work, or failure to achieve a personal goal can all produce crankiness in my life. Whether your temper flares and you raise your voice, or you cry tears of frustration, your baby will be listening through it all. You know what, though? Your little one is remarkably resilient. It's a lesson you should take to heart. You will make mistakes as a parent, but you should be willing to forgive yourself. Few people are as willing to let go of the past and simply love you for who you are—Mommy or Daddy—as your little one.

Rule 4: Your baby loves being held, but it won't hurt her to sit in a swing or lie on a play mat. If you are a first-time parent, you are especially vulnerable to the notion babies must be held around the clock. Although it's true skin-to-skin contact and up-close affection are critical for developing a bond with your baby, it's inaccurate to think you're a bad parent for occasionally placing her in a swing or laying her on a soft mat. Your baby's first days are limited by the fact that her vision hasn't yet fully developed. After the first few weeks, her vision begins to improve, which opens an entirely new world. Brain activity in babies suggests their waking hours are a little like wandering through a dream or a psychedelic trip, according to research reported in *The Wall Street Journal*.[14] By giving your baby new environments to explore and new stimuli such as a swaying swing or a rotating mobile, you are providing experiences that will inform her understanding of the surrounding world. It also enables you to finish a household chore, complete a meal, or simply take a short break.

Rule 5: You aren't the only person capable of helping your baby. As a parent, it's easy to think that letting a trusted friend or family member watch your child for a few hours as he gets older represents giving up responsibilities God gave you. The truth is it can be extremely beneficial to get away for a couple of hours, spend time with your spouse, and remember that you had a life, responsibilities, and hobbies before your little person arrived. If you know someone who will be an excellent caretaker for your child, arrange a date with your spouse or a handful of errands you can do without being away from your baby for too long. I'm not suggesting a two-week excursion while your baby is still nursing. Small outings will give you the outlet you need to enjoy time away from home without separating from your baby for an extended period of time.

Rule 6: Work will always be waiting for you. It's tempting to fret over all of the household tasks and workplace responsibilities you're missing by parenting your child. Let me assure you, those duties will never go away. People were engaged in those activities long before you arrived here, and those things will continue long after you are gone. If you ever get wrapped around the idea you're somehow failing because you didn't check a certain number of boxes that day, remember two things: First, you probably aren't the only person qualified to do the job. Second, the job will be waiting for you until you can complete it. Your child will only be a baby once, and the next 18 years or so are going to move rapidly. Savor each moment and each new phase of your child's development. You will never regret spending time with her. You might, though, regret neglecting time with your child so you could do something as pedestrian as spending excess time in the office or at home folding laundry.

Rule 7: Always let your moral compass guide your decisions, and always put your family near the root of your decision tree. If you are a Christian, your moral framework is the Bible and the instructions God has given all people for all time. Your role as a parent can serve as an extra layer to place over your decision-making processes. Remember the choices you make going forward not only affect you and your spouse but also your child. If something doesn't feel right, and it clearly violates the rules you have set for your family, don't do it. That includes making too many commitments on your time or sacrificing experiences with your growing family simply so you can satisfy another person's expectations of you. Unless that person is your spouse—in which case there's probably plenty of room to negotiate a choice that works for both of you—their needs are secondary to those of your immediate family. If someone else expects you to be at a meeting or an event, but it doesn't help your family or improve your relationship with them, be willing to sacrifice it.

Rule 8: Counterbalance your life versus balancing everything equally. In the business book *The ONE Thing*, authors Gary W. Keller and Jay Papasan argue that your life will never be a perfect balance of family and work life. Instead, life is a series of counterbalancing acts—at times, your family will take priority, such as on vacations; at other times, your work will have deadlines or big projects that must be completed, and an outsized portion of your time will be dedicated to your professional career. Earlier in this book, I shared how Julie and I took seasons of our life to prepare financially, whether saving for our adoption or getting out of student loan debt. The sacrifices in those stages were especially tough, and we often felt tempted to forego the plan for a night or two simply to recoup. Stick to your goals and good things will happen. It requires counterbalancing, but you'll be immensely satisfied with the outcomes that benefit you and your baby.

Rule 9: Give due respect to your elders. Whether you are talking to your grandparents and parents by phone or paying in person visits, there's no reason to rely simply on your own experiences for parenting wisdom. Multiple generations of your family have successfully raised children, and while you might not trust all of them equally for insights, chances are good you are close to a few of them whose experiences might make your life easier. Of course, you'll also have conversations that reveal how much parenting has changed.

I grew up drinking all kinds of orange and apple juice, and today's pediatricians don't typically recommend drinking much juice at all. But that's a very minor example compared to more valuable insights, such as older relatives who remind you how quickly your children will grow up, and how you should always take time to let your children know how proud you are of them. I once asked older friends I respect what they had observed about families whose children remained faithful Christians. They shared they had noticed those families tended to study the Bible together, in some form, every day, regardless of the circumstances. That led Julie and I to start our own daily Bible time with our children. Sometimes activities that seem small and insignificant can have the most powerful positive effect on our families.

Rule 10: You've only got one life, so use it wisely. You can't fight the fact there are 24 hours in a day, or the reality your newborn really must eat or sleep at regular intervals. Rather than shoving every daily experience into your mold of what convenient should look like, accept the fact that every day will be different—and "sufficient for the day is its own trouble" (Matthew 6:34).

Measure your success not by how many boxes you check each day but by the experiences you'll remember for the rest of your life. That sounds like a bunch of lame advice from a cheesy motivational speaker. But all the money or success in the world won't replace these special moments with your baby. Enjoy the journey, appreciate each moment (yes, even the boring or stressful or tedious ones), and remember you're building a reservoir of memories to draw on in the decades ahead.

The last advice I want to share, and one I have discovered while working on the manuscript for this book, is that you should always seek out people with a good sense of humor.

Julie and I are blessed with parents in arms here in our hometown and in places we've lived in the past. There's also a whole community of moms and dads living around the United States and in countries around the world, and you can tap into their collective wisdom via social media.

On Facebook, you can join private groups dedicated to helping adoptive families or families that are facing or have overcome infertility. You can use these groups to learn what other families are facing, share encouragement from your own experiences, or simply seek an outlet to share a difficult moment. On Twitter, parents sometimes use hashtags such as #momlife and #dadlife, and a whole bunch of others, to chronicle the funny things their children say, their shortcomings as parents, and the wins they've notched, small or big.

On all platforms, there are hundreds of parenting information outlets, free tools and tips, and other resources that can make you smarter and more resilient as a mom or a dad.

I wouldn't suggest letting social media or the online searches for parenting advice suck away precious hours from your life. Printed books or e-books can be a tremendous resource, as can time spent with loved ones who are actively parenting or those who have parented in the past. Your objective should always be to maximize your parenting outcomes for a minimal investment of time and energy. Your spouse and your children deserve most of that energy. And you know what? You deserve it too. Never forget what we discussed earlier in this book: in order to help your family be the best spouse and parent you can be, you must first help yourself.

Your adopted child, like any other children in your family, won't act or sound like you do. That's OK. The real question is whether he or she will grow up in a tight-knit home, surrounded by love, inspired by parents who care deeply and love openly. If you are doing those things, you will have done all that truly matters.

Discussion Questions

- Of the ten rules shared here, which most resonated with you? How will you modify your life to make sure you aren't setting expectations that are out of alignment with reality?

- What are some ways you can connect with and learn from other parents, both in your community and online?

- What is one step you will take this way to study the art of parenting?

- What is one activity you will sacrifice this week to ensure you have adequate time with your adopted baby and other children? Write it down and hand the note to your spouse or a trusted friend to serve as your accountability partner to ensure you meet that commitment.

17

THE PRINCESS ASCENDS HER THRONE

A babe in the house is a well-spring of pleasure, a messenger of peace and love, a resting place for innocence on earth, a link between angels and men.

—Martin Farquhar Tupper

In this chapter, you will learn

- How to enjoy to the fullest your baby's first months in your family
- Why your first baby will always hold a special place in your heart
- How you can capture your baby's early days without sacrificing all of your time to social media and scrapbooking

No matter how many children you have, you will always remember the milestones that your first accomplished. If your embryo baby is your family's first child, you will quickly discover that her every expression will become a subject of delight and a primary topic of conversation. This happens in your own house first, but it ripples outward to include your entire network of family and friends, far and wide.

Micah earned that status in our family. Our oldest little man entered the world when Julie and I were twenty-five, and he set a high bar for his brothers and sister. Julie and I are both the oldest of four children (Julie only by a few minutes, since she is a twin), so we have understood Micah's plight from the very beginning. On the one hand, he is a playful young man who enjoys a good game of Pokémon, a good wrestle on the floor with his little brothers, and the excesses of potty humor. On the other hand, he is a little leader whose obedience to his parents, kindness to his sister, and love for reading are mirror images of how Julie and I acted at that age.

There is something incredible about seeing yourself from a bygone era in the words and actions of your first baby, and you will invariably experience this too. Your baby might not hold a scrap of your genetic material, but you will surely see flashes of your own personality as she grows up. Let's not get too philosophical here, but there can be no mistaking we are all part of the family of humanity. There is something in our nature that ensures shared traits.

Be aware others might challenge your thinking on this. You will need to be prepared to throw up mental barriers if someone suggests your influence on your baby's character is slim to none. I have met people who believe all kinds of things about the way children develop, and based on my own experience, I encourage you to believe about 25 percent of it. There are generally a few schools of thought. I share them with you here not because I think you should believe them, but because you should be aware you will need to develop good comebacks for all of them if you don't buy into them (and usually, you won't).

For example, some people believe

- **Children are entirely at the mercy of their DNA.** This notion is supported by wild stories you read in *People* magazine about triplets who, separated tragically at birth, somehow managed to grow up with very similar traits, talents, and personal tics. I have to admit these stories are pretty striking. How is it that people raised in completely different households grow up to be so similar? Clearly, genetics are an important and lasting factor in our lives. It's why you are engaged in an open adoption so your child can build strong bonds with her placing family. To be clear, open adoption isn't only about building genetic relationships but expanding the loving kindness to which your baby is exposed. Your child's placing family loved her before she ever came into your life. At the same time, the notion genetics is everything conveniently ignores the 18-plus years you will spend raising each child. The average American lives to approximately age seventy-nine, meaning you will have a powerful role for nearly one-quarter of your child's life, and presumably long after that. In keeping with the theme of this chapter, let's not abdicate the throne just yet, parents. You might be raising a princess or a prince, but you're squarely seated on the throne until the generational transition of power occurs. Genetics matter a lot, but they're not the only factor at play here.

- **Children are entirely at the mercy of their environment.** This scenario is the opposite of the first, and it's equally flawed, if you ask me. I think it often stems from our insecurities as parents. When our children act out at home, or misbehave in public, we tend to point the finger of blame squarely at ourselves. Is this fair? Yes and no. On the one hand, you will find with your first child that you are more likely to have the time to devote to character development. If your baby tries to touch a hot burner on the stove, you're probably going to leap into action to ensure that she is safe and that she gets a little lecture on the dangers of heated objects. But if you desire to build your family, and you have other children in the future, you will find your time increasingly fragmented, which limits your ability to provide as much one-on-one attention as you once did.

Even more than that, your younger children's behavior will be guided by other influences, including older children. Your babies will find shortcuts. If you are giving your oldest child attention, your youngest might begin to throw a fit or do something risky to divert your precious time and care. I'm not at all suggesting children are dangerous imps bent on testing your every ounce of patience, though they certainly can be. Instead, I am suggesting that the environment you create for your family can, indeed, result in behavior change. But giving these conditions all of the power in your life places all of the burden squarely on your shoulders and those of your spouse, and that's not fair to you.

If you've ever seen children interacting on a playground, you know just as well as I do that you can pick out personality types from a mile away. Some are bossy, others immediately defer to the bossy types, and some simply fight the status quo. There's no question upbringing plays a role in these attitudes that are hilarious to observe at life's youngest stages, but there's also no dispute that at least a portion of these behaviors are deeply ingrained in our genetics.

- **Children are a hopeless mess of influences, including DNA and home environment, and we'll never change it, so why bother?** This is more or less the place where I've decided to set up camp in my own parenting journey. If you are a first-time parent, this is in no way meant to discourage you. Instead, I think it gives you a fair amount of grace for the journey that lies ahead. Each child is a precious gift, and regardless of her quirks, her life matters and she can do immense good for the world with the proper training. The activities she gravitates toward, the way she smiles, the words she uses, the generosity she demonstrates toward others—all of those things, from my experience, are a tightly woven combination of generations of genetics and also the short-term cultivation of parents who love her and seek to mold her character into something that will serve her well for a lifetime.

You should use this knowledge to celebrate your child's unique gifts while recognizing your own limitations as a parent.

I'm not suggesting that you check out and take an impromptu island vacation in Mallorca, Spain, while your baby runs your financial affairs back home and keeps a careful eye on your estate, though that would be awesome. What I'm encouraging you to do is to celebrate the experience of being a parent for the very first time. I realize some of you who are reading this probably have several kids like I do.

Regardless of where you are at in your journey, there are too many people out there claiming to have the ultimate keys to parenting success, and the majority of it is what we once called snake oil. It sounds amazing, it claims to cure all of our ills, and it's probably just diluted sugar water.

At the same time, there are a handful of experts who can help you maximize the early days of your parenting experience.

One of them is Dr. Meg Meeker, a longtime pediatrician who has written some great books including *Hero,* about being the father your children need, and *Strong Fathers, Strong Daughters,* which explains plainly the forces that threaten our daughters and the ways dads can help guide their steps and safeguard their purity. Dr. Meeker writes from a Christian perspective, and I've found her voice refreshing and easy to understand. You will find she is a great coach and a tremendous source of encouragement when you're having a rough day. Subscribe to her podcast, *Parenting Great Kids,* to hear from experts she thinks will make you a smarter parent.

Your first child will create many memories, and you will feel as if your only role in life is to document her every move.

Because I know you already are guilty of this—your iPhone is probably running at a turtle's pace under the weight of thousands of photos and hundreds of adorable baby-language videos—I want to assure you that you can take a deep breath and push Pause. Your quest to become the world's first dual parent-documentarian is noble. Your red-carpet premiere will probably feature dozens of your closest friends and family sitting around your living room and eating popcorn.

But the most important part of your parenting journey at this early stage is to live in the moment without the guilt of needing to capture every second on camera. Oh, you will feel the weight of failing to have your camera rolling when something cute happens. I've felt it before, especially with our middle sons, Titus and Ezra, who did not have the benefit of my full filmmaker attention as they grew up. Life gets busier and more complex as new young people arrive and begin demanding basic rights, such as food and clothing. Under the pressure of these little lobbyists, life becomes a game of grabbing juggling balls in midair and tossing them back to your spouse in a furious game of Don't Drop the Ball.

Spoiler alert: You will eventually drop the ball. And when you do, I want you to have the confidence of knowing which balls are acceptable to drop. First and foremost is the precious and culturally unacceptable duty of chronicling your child's every word, step, and mishap.

Here is how some parents I know have handled the transition from capture everything to capture only the most meaningful, as time allows. Julie has made it a point of writing a journal to each child in his or her first months. As you can imagine, each successive journal is a little thinner. Raising more little ones means more demands on your time and less opportunity to focus attention solely on one child. But the sentiment and the value those journals will bring one day can't be understated. Your baby will remember you when you are long gone, not because of all the photos and videos you took but because of the memories you created together and the safe environment you created in your home.

An editor of mine once explained to me her family's tradition, which is to take an annual family photo and place it alongside the year's major accomplishments for each family member. By focusing on an annual highlights reel versus a daily list-making session, this family reserved its time for the most important activity of all: living life together and then documenting a year's worth of memories before the start of the next 12 months.

I know these nice stories I've shared won't convince you entirely, so it will be up to you to fight the urge to keep up with your friends and family on social media.

There are plenty of times each week I use social media personally and professionally. It's fun to see what my loved ones are doing in other states and countries. I enjoy looking at beautiful European vistas. I like imaging how my life could be better if I knew how to make fancy food, or how to make a cat dance, or how to climb a building using only my fingers and a pocket knife.

But precious few of the discoveries I have made on social media, or the things that I have shared there, will change the world. Don't get me wrong. Social media presents an incredible platform for exchanging ideas, reflecting kindness, and building community. At the same time, it will never replace face-to-face relationships until the day we all decide to upload our minds to the cloud and create virtual thought forms of ourselves to float like ghosts through life. I'm pretty confident that will never happen.

If you're reading this 200 years in the future, and you are a virtual thought-form ghost, please accept my apologies. Until then, all of you parents need to take a step back and put your phone down. As fun as it is to share the latest video of your child doing something cute, it's more fun to enjoy the experience and keep it to yourself.

Wow, you're probably thinking to yourself, *this guy is not only a bad writer—he's also a jerk.*

Yes to both. But how often are you going to experience

your child's first word, or her first steps, or her first slobbery kiss from a favorite pet dog? The answer is never. I'll forgive you if you want to document some of those moments with a box made from glass and plastic, but I'm telling you that you will never regret putting down those devices and simply being in the moment.

This isn't a plea to embrace the mindfulness philosophy, in which somehow the embrace of meditation and transcendent peace of mind will guide you to your true north. It's simply a statement of fact. You only get so many hours in the day, and if you are like the most of the world and must earn a living to put food on the table and a roof over your head, you can't afford to squander those precious moments.

Remember what we said earlier: You are in a daily battle for your child's well-being, and it's up to you to find your motivations, rekindle the fire that led you on your adoption journey, and seize every waking moment. This isn't only about you and your desire to keep up with other people any more. It's about laying a foundation on which your child can be a life. You can chase your career, or the approval of others, or the next big purchase or vacation. At the end of your life, though, you'll have a bunch of hollow promises and little to show for them. Instead, I want to encourage you to pour yourself into your family—because family means you personally are worth an investment—and see where it takes you.

In no time at all, your child will go from being a few days old, to a few weeks, and then a few months.

As your embryo baby grows up, she will begin to interact with you even more. Today, Phoebe looks nothing like the photos our friend Vicki captured just a few days after returning home from the hospital. Yet somehow, she is more precious with each day that passes. Her babbles, coos, and squeals are filled with excitement. Phoebe isn't yet able to speak in a language we understand, but we love her words all the same. She has all the independence, fire, and life that our boys have. She will grow up to fight for the values she believes in, to love those around her, and to chart a course that is entirely her own.

As parents, Julie and I have the privilege of jogging alongside her and her brothers as they pick up speed down the runway. In a few short years, the din that consumes our house today will fall silent, and we will be left wondering how time got away from us.

Rather than regretting lost opportunities to spend time with our children, we have made it a point to put family at the center of everything I do. It is a line we have drawn not in the sand but in the bedrock. Anyone or anything that dares to step over the line will swiftly be pushed back into its place.

You went on the embryo adoption journey because you believed that one day, you would meet a beautiful baby who would change your world. She did. Now, build for her the life you have always imagined, with all its imperfections.

Discussion Questions

- How much of your embryo baby's personality will be determined by her genetics compared to her environment, in your view? Think about the experiences that have shaped your beliefs about childhood development, and be prepared to give yourself plenty of grace, knowing each baby is complex and special.

- What kind of an environment are you building for your child? Identify at least three character traits for the home you are creating, such as love, respect, patience, persistence or hopefulness.

- Where will you invest time in capturing memories of your embryo baby's early years? Alternately, where will you deliberately stop trying so hard to document every moment so you can celebrate life's special moments in real time?

18

TINY VICTORIES

*When you hold your baby in your arms the first time and
you think of all the things you can say and do to influence
him, it's a tremendous responsibility. What you do with him
and for him can influence not only him, but everyone he
meets and not for a day or a month or a year but for time
and for eternity.*

—ROSE KENNEDY

In this chapter, you will learn

- Why you should never lose sight of the road you have traveled on your embryo adoption journey

- How to celebrate what you and your now-extended family have accomplished so far, starting at your baby's earliest stage of life

- How you can use your unique talents and relationships to inspire other families to consider embryo adoption

Sometimes, seemingly tiny decisions have enormous consequences. My dad might not realize it, but his decision to unwaveringly read *The Denver Post* and *The Rocky Mountain News* as I was growing up led me to become a journalist. I can remember many nights when Dad, inspired by something he had read, brought a newspaper clipping to the dinner table to provide a dash of humor or a dose of common sense. I recall one night when Dad read a short clipping about families facing the terrible strain of the housing crisis. He concluded with a call and response.

"What should you always do?" Dad asked.

"Get a fixed-rate mortgage," my siblings and I responded, probably in deadpan fashion. (I know. It's not as if Dad tipped us off to the location of El Dorado or to Amelia Earhart's final port of call. But seriously, that advice has been a blessing. Compound it over many other nuggets of wisdom and you can see that reading the newspaper pays enormous dividends. Try it sometime if you aren't already.)

The same is true for my mom. She probably doesn't realize that her passion for writing—as evidenced by her professionally published articles of her growing-up years in the South, as documented in the letters she has written friends and family over decades—has inspired her children with a hunger for clear communication. Most of us no longer write printed letters (well, except for Mom and Dad), but my siblings and I fire emails back and forth weekly, and we like to keep our parents looped in.

The seemingly small seed of an idea, planted years in the past, can grow into a tall and sturdy tree of opportunity for all who have the privilege of passing beneath its shade.

This is precisely the way I want you to think about your embryo adoption. In a very real sense, the new branch you have added to your family tree is going to grow, flourish, and develop into something you never would have dreamed about in times past.

At our home in northeast Missouri, silver maple trees tower over our yard. In a storm last night, branches fell, and they will litter the yard this morning. But the roots of the trees remain firmly planted in the ground, and the trees have survived to continue telling their stories.

The apostle Paul spoke of God's ability to graft people into the tree of his church (Romans 11:17–24). The same can be said for God's ability to graft your embryo baby into a family that, while not related to her by blood, will love her more than she can possibly imagine.

All of those strong family ties are possible because of the journey you have taken in recent months. If you have used this book as a tool of encouragement along the way to a successful embryo adoption, you have a lot to celebrate. If you have used it as an opportunity to consider whether embryo adoption is right for you, perhaps your journey is just beginning. In either case, you have taken the time to become better informed and have expressed a deep interest in becoming a better parent. Good for you. Parenting is much more of an art than a science, no matter what others might claim.

Allow me to share an anecdote from my storied past as an inept parent. Someone once pulled me aside after Sunday morning worship services to share that God gives children padding on their backsides for a reason, and that reason is this: failure to paddle your children means they will grow up to make a mess of things. Perhaps you have heard this before. It certainly wasn't the first time I had heard a person champion the biblical principle that "folly is bound up in the heart of a child, but the road of discipline drives it far from him" (Proverbs 22:15).

The subtext of the comment, of course, was that my own child had been charged with misbehaving—and getting away with it. I smiled and managed to grumble something that sounded halfway appreciative for the observation. Then I reflected on the countless times I had disciplined the son in question only to face the same recurring issue of flat-out naughtiness.

Have you known children like that? Based on my assessment in that case and in many others since, I made the scientific determination that 94 percent of all parenting advice actually only works for the child of the person giving the advice. The remaining six percent falls within the margin of error.

You will encounter plenty of tough moments as you are raising your baby. Our oldest son, Micah, is now seven, and even in that narrow window of time we have experienced the challenges of parenting. These include the daunting task of finding disciplinary tactics that work for each child's personality, the hurtfulness of a child's unintentionally unloving words, and the exhaustion of negotiating bedtime terms when we feel ready to collapse.

You should know that those tasks are worth the fight, no matter how difficult they seem at the time. The truth is the moments are fleeting, and even the most protracted battles will eventually come to an end. Some people have attempted to capture the brevity of a child's time at home by creating a big glass jar with 6,570 marbles representing each day from birth until age 18. Others use 936 pennies, one for each of the weeks within the same time frame.

I don't like this approach for several reasons, and I would like to suggest an alternative when I am done complaining. First, the idea of tracking your child's every day is a bit like me tracking my lifespan with marbles. The idea is depressing. I can read daily reminders of the mortality of mankind in the news without bringing a glaring reminder into my own home.

My second beef is that your influence as a parent is only beginning in the first 18 years. I understand all of the reasons we view it as so critical. Never again will we have the opportunity to shape and mold our children's perspective of the world like we will when they are living under our roof. Will your influence as a parent vanish on your daughter's eighteenth birthday, much as Cinderella's carriage collapsed into a pumpkin at midnight? Absolutely not.

In my view, the relationship you build with your children should be so secure and lasting that it extends to the very edges of your lifetime. Few things are more tragic in my mind that parents and children who have drifted apart with no visible path to restoring their relationship. I realize all kinds of factors are out of your control and mine, but I've seen ample evidence in the lives of people I love to believe a lasting relationship is achievable.

I don't want you to go buy a marble-laden glass jar—an invitation for your curious children to smash it to pieces all over the floor—or to lug pennies around your house. Instead, if you want a powerful visual image of how your children are growing up, I have a recommendation. Watch your babies as they sleep at night. In our home, I have need only to walk in the evening into my sons' room, where they share a triple bunk bed, and watch them as they sleep. Their faces are maturing, their bodies are growing taller, and their ability to set goals and find their passion and ask smart questions increases daily. I'd rather see physical proof they are becoming little adults than obsess over little balls of glass.

This exercise will allow you to forget for a moment all of

those difficult parts of parenting—you know, the parts that really matter, where you build character—and to think a bit further ahead. Imagine the outcome of all those decisions.

The vision that alternately delights and terrifies me is the one where I walk down the aisle with my daughter on her wedding day. I am hopeful that on that day, all of the investment Julie and I have made in love, energy, and time will be rewarded with pure joy. The same can be said for our three sons on their big days. I hope all four of our children have strength of character and a brightly glowing future at the point when they choose to settle down. Sure, none of us always knows exactly where we are going. Yet the older we grow, the more our path becomes defined. I want to be part of that journey with my children because my parents traveled the same road with me.

You have an incredible opportunity to cast a vision for the future into the life of your adopted son or daughter.

As I grew up, my dad routinely spent time during family prayers asking that God would direct me and my siblings to find good Christian spouses. I didn't fully appreciate what he was doing at the time. Why ask God to arrange marriages that wouldn't happen for years down the road?

The answer to that question is far clearer after close to 11 years of marriage to Julie. My dad didn't make his petition simply so God would check the religion box on our "So You Think You Should Marry This Person?" scorecard. Instead, his request delved far deeper. He sought to ensure we would share a common faith, a common direction, and a common purpose. That foundation would form the basis for our entire married relationship and also for any children that would come from that relationship. Failure to create a solid base too often leads to shaky outcomes (Matthew 7:26).

You can give your adopted children similarly clear hints about where they are going. For example, you can make the following clear to them:

- **They are as much a part of your family tree and heritage as any other family member.** Although you will always celebrate, honor, and talk about their special adoption story, they are no different in another sense than any other family member. They are deserving of all of the rights and privileges of any other child with your family's last name.

- **They have as many paths to success as any other family member.** There is nothing about the act of embryo adoption that causes your child to miss out on life's biggest opportunities. All children can achieve big dreams, regardless of gender, socioeconomic status, special needs, or other factors. You should regularly explain to your children how proud you are of who they are and of how they are growing and maturing.

- **They will always be able to lean on you. In some cases, adopted children grow up feeling a gulf of separation between themselves and the adults in their lives.** They understandably experience feelings of loss and grief over the loss of deep relationships with their genetic family and feelings of hurt toward their adoptive parents. After all, their adoptive family in a sense pulled them away from their genetic family. Your child might experience some of these feelings, and I am under no illusions that my daughter might do the same. I want you to affirm your child's right to experience whatever emotions she might face while also making it clear you will always be there for her. Adoption brings great joy but also acute pain for placing families and adopting families alike, depending on life's season. Prepare your family for some difficult days along the way, but ensure you construct a foundation of love that will provide lasting support to your child.

- **They will always be a person of inherent value.** Our culture too often treats people as political footballs whose existence should be subjected to vigorous debate in the halls of Congress, on social media, or at the Supreme Court. Let me be clear: There is no higher authority than God's. If your family does not adhere to a Christian point of view, you may disagree with me. My perspective, cultivated over years of study and experience, leads me to believe that a fundamental reality of life is the inherent worth of every person. The spectrum of life begins with a one-cell zygote, then an embryo, then a fetus, and finally a newborn.

  There are many people who believe the idea that embryos are people is dangerous because it is a barrier to scientific discoveries that could help people who already have been born and are suffering from conditions for which we do not yet have a cure. I empathize strongly with people from all walks of life, especially those whose health is compromised and who are dependent on science and medicine to enjoy life to the fullest extent as I have. At the same time, I am convinced there are scientific breakthroughs yet available to us that would not force us to decide between using remaining embryos for research or bringing those embryos to term. As a society, we must foster a culture of adoption for all existing embryos without creating new ones that will never know the love of a family. Each embryo is a person, and as a society, we must reject anything that jeopardizes their safety and security.

- **They will always be within arm's reach of you and your spouse.** Your adopted child should have confidence that no matter what happens, the door will always be wide open to a full and fulfilling relationship with you. You might not be able to communicate this idea in meaningful words until your child is older. But you can work each day to show by your example how much he is loved and how deeply you desire to help and support him. Every passing day is a new chance to show affection, to celebrate your child, and to discover something new and wonderful about each other.

Never let a day pass without letting your child know where you stand on at least one of the points I've just outlined. In fact, you will probably find it hard *not* to talk about these truths each day. More than ever, that's exactly what our young people need: truth. How many people do you know, in public or private life, who have been caught in a lie they perpetuated? By telling your children in clear terms where you stand and what you believe about them, you are teaching them the honest truth about how they should view themselves. Society doesn't have permission to dictate the terms of their world. Neither do politicians or activists or authors who look like they just graduated middle school. (I've come to terms with my boyish charm.) If God created you, he gets to author your life plan. Everyone else can fall into line.

Your responsibility as an adoptive parent extends beyond your children to the many other people who are part of your life.

If you and your spouse decide to adopt embryos, you have made a very public and powerful statement about the value of life. This is true even if some or all of those embryos are not carried to term. As a result, you are now tasked with teaching others about embryo adoption.

Notice I didn't say, "You are now tasked with convincing others that your position is the right position." The only way you will ever change another person's mind is to lead by example and to cultivate influence by doing exactly the kinds of things good and decent parents do. There will always be people who believe embryo adoption is morally wrong, just as you believe it is morally necessary. You should always act and teach from a position of love and compassion. You should always be willing to listen and engage in thoughtful conversation and even debate without compromising your beliefs.

As a high school newspaper editor, I frequently wrote editorials that today cause me to cringe. The positions I took too often were black and white when reality is often gray or, more accurately, muddy. Looking back, I wish I could have acted with more empathy in the public discourse that shaped my early opportunities to influence others.

Now, I have a chance to modify my approach to the world, and so do you. Embryo adoption has permanently changed your family tree and given you a platform to share your child's story with others. What would your life be like without the baby you love? Advocacy is rarely a silent endeavor, though it can be powerful when done by disciplined and loving men and women.

Perhaps your embryo adoption story will be the catalyst that shapes another family's destiny. The only way you will ever know is to tell it.

Discussion Questions

- Whether you decide to use a jar of marbles or pennies, or simply reflect regularly on your child's limited time in your home, find a way to appreciate how your baby is growing up. How will you use the reality of your limited time together to shape his or her early years in a positive way?

- What affirmations can you use with your embryo baby to explain her inherent value and her place in your family's life and future? Write down three statements you will repeat to your child as she grows up to highlight the core values you wish to instill in her.

- How will you use your own talents and relationships to share the hope of embryo adoption with others?

AFTERWORD

Sometimes, a difficult journey is worth taking. This is especially true when the life of a fellow human being is the central focus.

My journey began with disbelief and skepticism about embryo adoption and ended with the daughter I had always dreamed about. Finally, our testosterone-filled household had a little lady to counterbalance the rough and tumble. For our placing family, the journey began with devastating health complications and overwhelming emotion and ended with the momentous decision to place embryos with a family they had never even met. They saw the potential for a lifelong relationship because of Julie's ability to bring a baby to term and because of our chicken-licking, mud-loving band of boys.

Your own story will be entirely different and entirely special. You will question what you are doing, grieve over losses big and small, pray for the outcomes you desperately desire, and celebrate the successes along the way. Each successive victory will be more meaningful than the last.

At the heart of it all will be your little boy or girl, the one whose origin story is heroic in a way few can claim. Frozen embryos aren't simply a statistic and a by-product of our ability to formulate life in a laboratory. They are evidence that you and I can make a profound impact on the world around us if we begin with the premise that each person, no matter how small, has inherent worth.

The cover of this book features our daughter, Phoebe. My wonderful cover artist prepared a handful of these cover options, and Julie and I asked family and friends to share which version they liked best. In one, Phoebe is lying on the bed, her face down and betraying a shy grin. In the other, Phoebe has her head held high and is staring directly into the camera, little fingers in the background and those big doe eyes in the foreground.

The vote ended up splitting about evenly down the middle. Everyone agreed both would work well. Some thought the first version with the grin gave a sense of gentleness and personality. Others said the version where she stares at the reader pulls at your heartstrings and urges you not to forget about her and babies like her.

I couldn't shake that image from my mind. The book needed to clearly challenge its readers: How can you deny the worth of a child who, after years in subzero temperatures as a handful of cells, now has the opportunity to experience life and all of its wonder? Yes, there will be heartache and pain. Yes, there will be moments of difficulty.

But Phoebe will also laugh uproariously as Titus takes the corners of his stuffed-animal blankets in his hands and spins them like wind turbines. She will absorb the wonder of chickens and of the woods surrounding our home. She will experience the simple joy of a home-cooked meal, of a ride on the school bus, and of tea parties with friends.

I hope that one day, she will experience the blessing of marriage and the gift of children all her own.

Phoebe's journey began with two steps: a loving family's decision to place her for adoption and our decision to adopt her. It's my hope this book will provide the road map you need to take one of the most meaningful steps of your lifetime too.

Our world's frozen embryos can become men and women who are a powerful force for good. It's up to us to give them a fighting chance.

ACKNOWLEDGMENTS

I owe sincere thanks to many wonderful, talented, and compassionate people for helping me bring this book to life. My three sons—Micah, Titus, and Ezra—instructed me in the joy of parenting and helped me bottle it for others. The amazing Snowflakes® Embryo Adoption team at Nightlight® Christian Adoptions and the fabulous team at Missouri Center for Reproductive Medicine kept Phoebe safe at her tiniest stages and brought her into our lives with a clear path for the future.

Kassidy, Kallie, and Kaiden Schmidt welcomed us into their family. Dennis and Janie Steele provided ongoing spiritual guidance, life coaching, and unlimited child care. Curt Harding generously read my book proposal and gave keen recommendations that took the project from concept to bookshelf. Carla Bale came up with the beautiful title.

Larry Carpenter and his team at Carpenter's Son Publishing opened my eyes to the world of publishing and delivered unbelievable support at every stage of the process. Tammy Kling shared my passion for this topic and turned text on paper into a compelling story. Suzanne Lawing designed the heart-melting cover. (Yes, that's Phoebe!) Greg Gaia gave my early chapters a tremendous copyedit and helped refine my thinking about my audience.

My comrades in arms at Trust In Food™ and Farm Journal encouraged me as I worked on this project in my off-hours. My Social5 friends paved the runway so I could transition from four amazing years of freelance writing to book writing. My first librarian crush, Mrs. Fryberger at Longmont Estates

Elementary, fed my hunger for reading with a smile.

My grandpa, James King, taught me the value of personal development and often reminded me that one of my earliest requests of him was, "Grandpa, tell me a story." Longtime friends Kaye and Bill Adams, and Ray and Kay Findley, taught me to treasure life because it is too short to squander.

I've undoubtedly failed to name many others. I thank God for all of you.

Embryo adoption brings together placing families such as the Schmidts and adoptive families such as the Birts with the best interest of children at heart. In the back row from left are John Schmidt and "Frozen, But Not Forgotten" author Nate Birt. In the middle row from left are Kassidy Schmidt, Kris Schmidt, embryo baby Phoebe Birt, Julie Birt, and Micah Birt. In the front row are Kallie Schmidt, Kaiden Schmidt, Titus Birt, and Ezra Birt. The parents managed to pull their children away from playtime in the fall leaves long enough to snap this photo on Sunday, October 28, 2018. Photographer: Bruce Van Hook

Appendix A

COMMON QUESTIONS AND ANSWERS ABOUT EMBRYO ADOPTION

You will find that while many people have questions about embryo adoption, several are especially common. Use the information on the following pages to help you respond to the curious, the worried, and the skeptical. I hope you will also subscribe to my weekly email newsletter, which contains my blog posts on embryo adoption and parenting, links to free resources I've put together, and content from experts you should follow. To subscribe, visit www.frozenbutnotforgotten.com.

What exactly is embryo adoption, anyway?

Embryo adoption is the process of bringing two families together for the purpose of bringing to term remaining embryos from the process of in vitro fertilization (IVF). The adoption process for embryos came about as an effort to ensure any babies born through embryo adoption would have the validation of being cared for in a way similar to other forms of adoption, such as domestic and international. Families seeking to place or adopt embryos should keep in mind that the primary focus of their efforts should be giving embryos the best chance at life and ensuring these children know they are loved by their adoptive family. In cases of open adoption, it is important for children to have some degree of connection with their placing family. This decision is up to you as a parent and should be made in the best interest of your child.

How does embryo adoption work?

The adoption process varies depending on your agency, but typically it will involve a variety of phone calls, paperwork, a legal contract, home studies, correspondence with the placing family, and more. Once the adoption papers are completed, your adopted embryos will be shipped to your fertility clinic in preparation for the embryo transfer. The transfer involves the process of a doctor placing one or more embryos into the woman's uterus for the purpose of carrying them to term. Families generally participate in an adoption that is open to some degree. This means your adopted baby will know her genetic family's medical history as well as have the opportunity to build an ongoing relationship throughout her life. Some families choose closed or even anonymous adoption.

What are the risks of embryo adoption?

The risks of embryo adoption extend not only to adoptive circumstances but to all pregnancies. For example, there is no guarantee an embryo will survive the thawing process, which could mean no babies are born from the process. The same is true for pregnancy, where numerous complications can arise. Other risks can include failing to match with a placing family that has remaining embryos. If a couple is too mature in age or already has a number of other children, it is possible an agency will decline placement. The best place to start is to do your research and to have a conversation with an adoption agency or fertility clinic you trust to begin exploring whether embryo adoption is right for you.

What are the arguments against embryo adoption and for it?

Embryo adoption opponents often state that such adoptions prevent valuable scientific study, such as embryonic stem cell research, from continuing. The unique physiological properties of embryos make them ideal for identifying new cures for diseases that people who already have been born are enduring. Others believe an embryo is not a human. Some theologians believe the popular Christian perspective that life begins at conception is a flawed reading of ancient biblical texts. They argue that the authors of Scripture didn't have today's scientific insights into the process of human development and that those writers understood the process of ensoulment happens later on in a baby's growth in utero, or that the process is simply a mystery. Yet others argue that by bringing embryos to term, couples are exposing them unnecessarily to the suffering and pain all too common to our world, or effectively promoting the use of IVF.

Embryo adoption proponents argue each embryo represents a unique human life. Those who see the world through a Christian perspective often argue each person reflects God's divine image and that God has given each person a unique set of talents and abilities to help the people around him or her. By bringing embryos to term, couples will have the opportunity to raise children who might help solve our world's most pressing problems, whether finding the cure for cancer, leading nations, or engaging in any number of other beneficial activities. Rather than viewing embryo adoption as a process that encourages more families to use IVF, those who support embryo adoption see it as a way to protect and bring to term remaining children conceived through assisted reproductive technology. They point out many couples using IVF often are unaware they will have remaining embryos. The adoption process is an opportunity to bring together loving families for the purpose of nurturing children from the very earliest stages of life.

Is embryo adoption legal?

Yes, embryo adoption is as legally binding as any other form of adoption. Although embryos are considered property in most US states, there are states such as Louisiana that have taken steps to codify a fact the Bible already makes clear: embryos are humans from the very moment of conception. Contracts vary depending on your circumstances. Common elements include statements acknowledging that the adopting family will do everything in its power to bring the embryos to term, that the families will maintain contact on a mutually acceptable level in cases of open adoption, and that the placing family will be kept up to date about the progress of the embryo transfer and any pregnancies and delivery.

Some adopting families worry about the possibility of a placing family taking back their baby after he or she is carried to term. To my knowledge, there is no legal precedent for such an action taking place. It is true there are occasionally high-profile disputes about which member of a separated couple retains the legal right to frozen embryos, but those situations are case dependent. It is my hope that Americans will set aside political divisions on this issue. Every embryo is a person, and every person deserves the full protection of our law, the love of a family, and the right to life.

Appendix B

MORE EMBRYO ADOPTION RESOURCES

Whether you are thinking about adopting embryos, in the middle of the adoption process, or continuing your education as an adoptive parent, the internet has many helpful resources on this important topic. You can visit my website (**www.natebirt.com**) for a list of links I think are particularly valuable, and you can also perform an online query by typing "embryo adoption" into your favorite search engine. Here are some helpful pages that will get you started:

Dreaming Of Diapers (dreamingofdiapers.com) shares one woman's experience with infertility, IVF, and finally family through surrogacy. Told from a Christian perspective and with refreshing honesty, this regularly updated blog will encourage couples who are facing infertility.

Embryo Adoption Awareness Center (www.embryo-adoption.org) is a hub for all families considering some aspect of the embryo adoption process. You'll find lists of embryo adoption agencies, a regularly updated blog, free webinars, videos, health insurance tips, lists of home study providers, and stories of families who have successfully adopted embryos.

Embryo Adoption Services of Cedar Park (www.adoptembryos.org and www.donateembryos.org) connects placing and adoptive families. I also recommend President and Co-Founder Maria D. Lancaster's book, *Souls On Ice,* for inspiring embryo adoption stories told through a Christian lens. Be sure to subscribe to the email newsletter, which includes recent photos and family adoption stories. It brings a smile to my face with every new edition.

My Little Soldiers (mylittlesoldiers.net) is specifically written for people experiencing male infertility by a man who has been through the pain himself. It provides valuable insights and firsthand anecdotes to provide couples with perspective and hope.

My Path to Mommyhood (mypathtomommyhood.blogspot.com) chronicles one couple's journey with infertility and the pain and joy along the way. It will help you appreciate the hope that exists for couples when children are not part of the path.

Open Hearted Open Adoption (www.openheartedopenadoption.com) shares author Lori Holden's adoption experience with practical wisdom for a successful open adoption.

Sacred Heart Guardians (www.sacredheartguardians.org) provides burial for embryos that do not survive the thawing process, with no fees required.

Sherrie Eldridge Adoption Blog (sherrieeldridgeadoption.blog) is a tremendous resource for families touched by adoption or foster care. You'll find wisdom for everything from helping children navigate school to searching for genetic families.

Snowflakes in the Rain (snowflakesintherain.blogspot.com) provides one family's challenges and joys while pursuing embryo adoption.

NOTES

[1] "Fertility & Infertility FAQ," American Pregnancy Association, http://americanpregnancy.org/infertility/fertility-faq/.

[2] Tian Zhu, "In Vitro Fertilization," The Embryo Project Encyclopedia, Arizona State University, July 22, 2009, https://embryo.asu.edu/pages/vitro-fertilization.

[3] Jeff Wang and Mark V Sauer, "In Vitro Fertilization (IVF): A Review of 3 Decades of Clinical Innovation and Techno-logical Advancement," *Therapeutics and Clinical Risk Management 2*, no. 4 (December 2006): 355–364, https://www.ncbi.nlm.nih.gov/pmc/articles/PMC1936357/.

[4] http://www.chicagotribune.com/news/sns-bc--ma-exchange-baby-bowl-20170925-story.html (site discontinued).

[5] "What Is Endometriosis? Causes, Symptoms and Treatments," The Endometriosis Foundation of America, https://www.endofound.org/endometriosis.

[6] "ART Success Rates," Centers for Disease Control and Prevention, https://www.cdc.gov/art/artdata/index.html.

[7] Saswati Sunderam et al., "Assisted Reproductive Technology Surveillance — United States, 2014," *Surveillance Sum-maries 66*, no. 6 (February 10, 2017): 1–24, https://www.cdc.gov/mmwr/volumes/66/ss/ss6606a1.htm.

[8] "ART Success Rates," CDC.

[9] Dawn Davenport, "How Many IVF Cycles Should You Try Before Giving Up?," Creating a Family, https://creatingafamily.org/infertility-category/how-many-ivf-cycles-should-you-try-before-giving-up/.

[10] Sarah Zhang, "A Woman Gave Birth From an Embryo Frozen for 24 Years," *The Atlantic,* December 21, 2017, https://www.theatlantic.com/science/archive/2017/12/frozen-embryo-ivf-24-years/548876/.

[11] Rachel Gurevich, "How Much Does IVF Really Cost?," Verywell, February 12, 2018, https://www.verywellfamily.com/how-much-does-ivf-cost-1960212.

[12] Amy Goldstein and Ariana Eunjung Cha, "Patients Mobilize after Malfunctions at Fertility Clinics Damage Thousands of Eggs, Embryos," *Chicago Tribune,* March 12, 2018, http://www.chicagotribune.com/news/nationworld/midwest/ct-damaged-embryos-ohio-hospital-20180312-story.html.

[13] "Infertility FAQs," Centers for Disease Control and Prevention, https://www.cdc.gov/reproductivehealth/infertility/index.htm.

[14] Alison Gopnik, "For Babies, Life May Be a Trip," *The Wall Street Journal,* July 18, 2018, https://www.wsj.com/articles/for-babies-life-may-be-a-trip-1531932587.